Nineteenth-Century Britain
1815–1914

Michael Willis

Blackwell Education

First published 1990
© Michael Willis

Published by Basil Blackwell Ltd
108 Cowley Road
Oxford OX4 1JF
England

British Library Cataloguing in Publication Data
Willis, Michael
  Reading historical documents: nineteenth-century
  Britain, 1815–1914.
  1. Great Britain, 1714 – Historiology
  I. Title
  941.07′072

  ISBN 0-631-90266-X (Non-net)
  ISBN 0-631-17596-2 (Net)

Typeset in Compugraphic Palacio by BP Integraphics Ltd, Bath
Printed in Hong Kong by Wing King Tong Company Ltd

Cover illustration by Max Beerbaum, reproduced with the permission of Eva Reichmann

Contents

Introduction

Nineteenth-Century Britain: 1815–1914 should help students to tackle the kind of document questions set in exams but we hope that this book will also serve a much wider purpose. The point of reading documents is not, after all, just to prepare for exams or answer a seemingly endless series of sterile comprehension questions. It is to allow the men and women of the past to speak to us. We must attempt to understand their value judgements, avoid labelling or dismissing them too readily and evaluate their arguments according to the state and society in which they lived.

Historical sources are also our means of answering questions about the past. Each sub-section of the book tackles some significant historical issue or question, but it should not be assumed that it can offer a neat answer. Rather, these sub-sections suggest something of the range and type of sources available which can help in providing an answer, and the problems involved in using them. Above all, it must be remembered that these sources are one editor's selection and that another editor might choose quite different sources which could suggest very different conclusions.

Each sub-section includes a set of questions. Some draw attention to phrases or extracts from the sources which are particularly difficult or significant, while others require the kind of summary, comparison and evaluation demanded in 'A' level exams, for example. Most of the question sets are also designed to develop one clearly specified line of inquiry. Many of the

sections contain detailed guidance on what to look for, but there are also standard questions which the historian must ask of any source. For example,

What kind of source is it? Is it, for instance, an extract from a law, a public speech, a novel or a private letter?

When was it written or produced?

What do we know about the writer or artist and his/her background? How may his/her upbringing, character, career and opinions have influenced what he/she writes or draws?

How well informed was the writer or artist?

Under what circumstances was the source produced? Who was it designed to influence and for what purpose? There is, for example, an enormous difference between a confidential letter intended for the eyes of only one person and a letter or statement written for publication.

These questions are not written out in every sub-section, but we must ask them to work out the significance of a source and what we can learn from it. We must also compare sources with careful attention to their differences and to the dates when they were written. Of course, we cannot always answer all our questions, but by thinking about them and investigating them we will move towards a more thorough understanding of the past.

Ideally, no doubt, we would work out all

historical problems by using sources from the period we are studying. Practically, of course, we cannot do all this ourselves and we thus have to rely on the work of others. Consequently, a range of historians' books must be used, and many of the sets of questions included in this book refer not just to the sources printed here but also to wider knowledge. Where such knowledge is required, reading references are given to a range of books which are likely to be available in schools and libraries. In a few cases, where a particular historiographical debate is mentioned, there are also references to the key historians' works, but generally the aim is to give a few guidelines for further inquiry and comparison, not a fully scholarly bibliography. All references are detailed in a separate 'Notes' section which can be found at the end of the sub-sections.

This book therefore launches a series of investigations into British life and government between the Napoleonic and First World Wars. This is an enterprise relevant not just to History students but to all who are interested in the evolution of modern Britain.

Michael Willis
Brentwood School, Essex

Acknowledgements

The author and publisher are grateful to the following for permission to reproduce illustrations:

Mary Evans Picture Library for pages 13 and 14
Hulton-Deutsch for pages 5, 22, 30 and 80
Illustrated London News Picture Library for pages 71 and 83
Punch for pages 55, 63, 99 and 109
Eva Reichmann for the cover

The author and publishers also wish to thank the following for permission to reproduce copyright material:

Edward Arnold for extracts from:
Anderson M S 1970 *The Great Powers and the Near East 1774–1923*
Baxter R D 1962 *Essays in Economic History*
Gash N 1968 *The Age of Peel*

The Athlone Press for extracts from:
Genville J A S 1964 *Lord Salisbury and Foreign Policy: The Close of the Nineteenth Century*

A & C Black for extracts from:
Bullock A, Shock M 1967 *The Liberal Tradition from Fox to Keynes*

Curtis Brown for extracts from:
Butler D, Freeman J 1963 *British Political Facts 1900–1960*

Cambridge University Press for extracts from:
Garrard J 1977 *Parties, Members and Votes after 1867: A Local Study*

Mitchell B R, Deane P 1971 *Abstract of British Historical Statistics*
Rimmer W G 1960 *Marshalls of Leeds, Flax Spinners 1788–1886*

Chatto and Windus for extracts from:
Read D 1973 *Documents from Edwardian England*

Collins for extracts from:
Wilson T 1966 *The Downfall of the Liberal Party 1911–1928*
Wilson T 1970 *The Political Diaries of C. P. Scott 1911–1928*

Essex Record Office for extracts from:
Brown A J F 1952 *English History from Essex Sources 1750–1900*

Eyre and Spottiswoode for extracts from:
Handcock W D 1977 *English Historical Documents 1874–1914*

Longman for extracts from:
Read D 1979 *England 1868–1914*

Macmillan for extracts from:
O'Day A 1979 *The Edwardian Age: Conflict and Stability 1900–1914*

Manchester University Press for extracts from:
Porter A N 1980 *Joseph Chamberlain and the Diplomacy of Imperialism 1895–99*

Odham Press for extracts from:
Briggs A 1968 *Victorian Cities*

Oxford University Press for extracts from:
Johnson N E 1981 *The Diary of Gathorne Hardy, Later Lord Cranbrook, 1866–1892*

viii *Acknowledgements*

Routledge for extracts from:
    Hollis P 1973 *Class and Conflict in Nineteenth Century England 1815–1850*
    Smith P 1967 *Disraelian Conservatism and Social Reform*

Simon and Schuster for extracts from:
    Wrigley C 1976 *David Lloyd George and the British Labour Movement*

Stanley Thornes for extracts from:
    Tames R 1971 *Documents of the Industrial Revolution 1750–1850*

1 Parliamentary Reform and Political Change

From medieval times through to 1832 the arrangements for electing the House of Commons changed little: they were characterised by local variation and based on tradition. In the century following 1832, elections were transformed to become substantially uniform and based on democratic principles. There is no doubt that the first Reform Act was crucial in opening the door to this change, but how did it come about?

There had been many proposals to reduce corruption and rationalise the system in the late eighteenth century, but with the French Revolution many came to regard even moderate ideas for constitutional reform as dangerous. By 1830 pressure and enthusiasm for reform were much increased and Lord Grey's new Whig ministry took up the issue from a debatable mixture of political conviction and hopes for parliamentary and party advantage.

Subsequent events were centred in Parliament and the outcome may be explained substantially in parliamentary terms. But there was public agitation at crucial points, and many have argued that it was the people rather than the politicians who carried reform. In particular there was well-publicised popular activity when the Lords rejected the government's second reform bill in October 1831 and later when they delayed its third bill in May 1832. This led to Grey's resignation and attempts by the Duke of Wellington to form an alternative government pledged to a weaker measure of reform. E P Thompson[1] perceived mass agitation by a newly emergent working class, and many historians have concluded that the situation was revolutionary. Alternatively, Professor Hamburger[2] has argued that intellectual radicals created a phoney impression of revolution. For example, the prominent radical Parkes was responsible for many of the newspaper reports of large meetings around Birmingham. Michael Brock in his authoritative book *The Great Reform Act*[3] concluded that agitation in May 1832 was the most intense that contemporaries had known but found it impossible to say whether the situation was revolutionary.

1.1 Was England Near to Revolution in the 'Days of May' 1832?

A *This extract is taken from a report in 'The Times' of a meeting held at Newhall-hill near Birmingham on 7 May 1832.*

Last Monday a meeting, undoubtedly the most numerous ever collected upon one spot for a political object, and which, notwithstanding the extraordinary greatness of its numbers, was remarkable for the unanimity and order of its proceedings, was held at Birmingham '... to assist in enabling our most excellent King, and his patriotic ministers, to accomplish their great measure of reform ...'

... the decided manifestation which the men of the midland counties gave on this occasion of their determination to support the Reform Bill, and not submit to any mutilation of its great provisions, will, we fancy, put to silence, for a short time, the Tory cry, so often raised and as often shown to be ridiculously unfounded, that 'the people are indifferent to reform.'

The meeting was assembled at the foot of Newhall-hill, a large piece of waste ground lying to the north of the town of Birmingham ... As each company entered Birmingham they were met by large bodies of the townspeople and loudly cheered. The different Political Unions having collected at the Birmingham Union Rooms, they moved off in procession to the place of meeting, where they arrived at a quarter to 12 o'clock; and some idea of their numbers may be conceived from the fact, that they continued to descend the hill in one dense and unbroken line from that time until 20 minutes past 12 o'clock, amidst the loud cheers of the people who had already collected there. At this moment there must have been upwards of 200,000 persons present, and in a short time the numbers were still further increased by the arrival of more unions. Beside this, numbers of people, who could obtain no place in the field, which was now completely filled, loitered about the neighbourhood, and thronged the streets of Birmingham.

The Times, 9 May 1832

B *A report of the same meeting in a letter from Reverend R L Freer to the Duke of Wellington.*

I arrived this morning from Birmingham ...

I reside as a clergyman within three miles of that town, and possess considerable means of knowing, and have indeed witnessed many of the proceedings in that place lately.

The first point of which I have to assure your Grace is that the boasted meeting of the political unions on this day week, and which has been cried up as consisting of 200,000 persons, never amounted to more than a *quarter* of that number; indeed I was assured by a gentleman who was present with a military officer, that he computed the whole assembly as never exceeding 30,000.

Another fact is, that at this moment Birmingham is far from being *radical*, the majority of respectable persons being decidedly *conservators* ...

In: Wellesley A R (ed.) 1880 *Despatches, Correspondence and Memoranda of Field Marshal Arthur Duke of Wellington K. G.*, Vol. 8, John Murray, pp 318–19

C *From 'Memories of the Reform Crisis' written by the radical J A Roebuck.*

... to attain our end, much was said, that no one really believed; much was done, that no one would like to own ... affairs never came to violence, though the danger was often threatened. In fact, often, when there was no danger, the cry of alarm was raised to keep the House of Lords and the aristocracy generally in what was termed a state of wholesome terror ... when some recalcitrant Tory attacked the Bill, when its provisions were threatened either with destruction or even mutilation, black clouds rose obedient to our call, as regularly as on the stage at the scene-shifter's command ... They who pulled the strings in this strange puppet-show were cool-headed, *retiring*, sagacious, determined men. *They* were never the noisy orators who appeared important, but were men studiously avoiding publicity; not that they wanted courage ... They directed everything, but never came before the public as leaders. They determined what meetings should be held, what resolutions should be proposed, who should preside, who should speak, and not seldom what should be said ...

'Life of an Old Politician.' In: *Bentley's Miscellany*, Vol. 23, 1848, p 521

D *This extract is taken from a government spy's report on the National Union of the Working Classes in London, 12 March 1832.*

... a person named Murphy who has been in the Cavalry of the Army agreed to learn any persons of the Union The Sword Exercise .. I find that as I have many times stated numbers of my associates are armed and are now quite eager to advise others to do so. I find too as I expected and stated that as the Fast Day [arranged for 21 March] approaches much anxiety exists among them ...

There is no organization in us as a body, but many do calculate that on that day we shall have "a good opportunity to do something." ... I agreed to meet some of our Class (73) on Sunday Morning to learn the Sword exercise . . . we went to Bartletts in Vine Yard, Vine St Spital-fields where we met Murphy [and others]. . . we all openly practised the exercise under Murphy who chalked on the wall the Six buts of a Circle as practised by the Army. We were about two hours at this and afterwards agreed to empower Murphy to take a Room which he knows in Goodmans Yard Minories at 2/- per week for our future practise, but we are to meet at Vine Yard again next Sunday . . .

PRO Home Office Papers 64/12

E *The Whig MP for Staffordshire, Sir John Wrottesley, speaking on the crisis in the House of Commons.*

. . . He had received a petition from Wolver-hampton, expressing, in very strong terms, the sentiments of the people respecting the course which their constituents wished that House to adopt in the present crisis . . . The neighbour-hood from which he had received the petition to which he had alluded was populous; and the greater part of the dense population depended upon their daily labour for their daily bread. In consequence of the situation of public affairs, a vast number of those people were thrown out of employment, and were in a state of the utmost destitution; and if measures were not taken to put an end to the stagnation of trade, and the want of confidence throughout the country, the people would be driven to acts which, without the excitement of the most galling distress, they would not be capable of committing.

Hansard, 17 May 1832. Ser. 3, Vol. 12: 1037–8

Questions

1 a What do you think the government spy meant by 'the Fast Day' (Source D line 7) and how would you explain its name?

b What was 'the situation of public affairs' to which Sir John Wrottesley referred (Source E line 10)?

2 Compare the accounts of the Newhall-hill meeting and the different opinions in Sources A and B. How far do they complement and how far do they contradict each other?

3 Consider the circumstances in which Sources A, B and C were written and the likely opinions and knowledge of the writers. How do these affect the use historians can make of the sources? How far should Source C affect the use we make of Source A?

4 What problems are there in using the government spy's account in Source D?

5 How usable is Sir John Wrottesley's statement in Source E as:

a evidence on the situation in the Midlands?

b evidence of the impact of popular agitation on Parliament?

6 Using these sources and any other available evidence how near do you think England was to revolution in May 1832?[4]

Notes

1 Thompson E P 1968 *The Making of the English Working Class* Pelican

2 Hamburger J 1963 *James Mill and the Art of Revolution* Yale University Press

3 Brock M 1973 *The Great Reform Act* Hutchinson

4 For further summary and discussion, see:
Thomis M I, Holt P 1979 *Threats of Revolution in Britain 1789–1848* Macmillan, Chap. 4
Stevenson J 1979 *Popular Disturbances in England 1700–1870* Longman, Chap. 10
Dinwiddy J R 1986 *From Luddism to the First Reform Bill* Blackwell, Chap. 3
Wright D G 1988 *Popular Radicalism* Longman, Chap. 5

1.2 The Impact of the First Reform Act – Elections Before and After 1832

The first Reform Act altered voting quali-fications substantially and redistributed parliamentary seats extensively, but how far did it change the conduct of elections where men still voted in public? Did it make them less corrupt?

One of the most famous descriptions of an early nineteenth-century election is Dickens' fictional account of the Eatanswill contest in *Pickwick Papers*. This was almost certainly based on an election he witnessed in the Suffolk borough of Sudbury in 1834. Yet Sudbury was far from being a typical borough. It had only just managed to keep its representation in 1832 and most of its electors gained the vote under a traditional qualification as freemen. In 1844 Sudbury was disenfranchised for gross bribery and corruption. It is possibly best seen as an extreme example of a number of small and rather rotten boroughs which survived from compromise arrangements in 1832.

A *The expenses of T B Lennard, a candidate in an uncontested election in the Essex borough of Maldon in 1830.*

	£	s	d
The Mayor for Hustings	100	–	–
Constables nominated by Committee	3	7	6
Chair Carriers	10	10	–
Borough Reeve	2	10	–
Flag Men	3	3	–
Band	10	10	–
Miss Burton dressing Chair	13	11	–
Youngman Printers Bill, Colchester Gazette Address	10	13	2
All Saints Church Ringers, Mr May fixed the sum	7	7	–
Saint Marys Church Ringers, Mr May fixed the sum	7	7	–
Whitmore White Hart	54	5	–
Dawson Chequers	70	18	6
Barker Rose & Crown	49	12	9
Cottee May Pole	21	1	6
Everard Lion	19	13	–
Cottee Bull	9	1	6

	£	s	d
Harris Bell	14	11	–
Barbrook Green Man	10	11	–
Shyn Blue Boar	1	17	6
Turner White Horse	6	7	10
Holloway Anchor	20	16	6
Ward Angel	–	11	–
Miles Rodney	1	10	8
Ainger Wellington	1	16	8
French Kings Head	69	19	–
Wright Attorney	10	10	–
Porter Check at one of the Public Houses	–	10	–
Dedman & Quilter Checks at Inns	1	7	6
Smith for Committee Rooms	10	10	–
Holland Check at Chequers Inn		17	6
Gisby at Leigh	7	4	6
Dyer making Chair	3	2	3
Sadd for Chair Stand	2	12	6
Curtis of Billericay	1	1	–
Expences paid by Mr. May	15	10	7
Turner Rochford delivering letters	1	3	6
Chig. Wire his Acc[oun]t	3	3	4
Servants at Kings Head	1	4	–
J. Payne paid postage for Circulars, and other Expences attending the Election	4	17	–
Archer Chelmsford delivering letters		5	–
Amount of Election Acc[oun]t	585	10	6

Essex Record Office D/DL 042/4

B *An election at Tonbridge, Kent, December 1832.*

J & C Dodd *View of Tonbridge During the Late Election, December 18th 1832*

C *This extract from Dickens' 'Pickwick Papers' gives a description of the contest between the Hon. Samuel Slumkey and Horatio Fizkin Esq. at Eatanswill.*

[Mr Slumkey's agent said] 'We have opened all the public-houses in the place, and left our adversary nothing but the beer-shops – masterly stroke of policy that, my dear sir, eh?' – the little man smiled complacently, and took a large pinch of snuff.

'And what are the probabilities as to the result of the contest?' inquired Mr Pickwick.

'Why doubtful, my dear sir; rather doubtful as yet,' replied the little man. 'Fizkin's people have got three-and-thirty voters in the lock-up coach-house at the White Hart.'

'In the coach-house!' said Mr Pickwick, considerably astonished by this second stroke of policy.

'They keep 'em locked up there till they want 'em,' resumed the little man. 'The effect of that is, you see, to prevent our getting at them; and even if we could, it would be of no use, for they keep them very drunk on purpose. Smart fellow Fizkin's agent – very smart fellow indeed.' . . .

During the whole time of the polling, the town was in a perpetual fever of excitement. Everything was conducted on the most liberal and delightful scale. Excisable articles were remarkably cheap at all the public-houses; and spring vans[1] paraded the streets for the accommodation of voters who were seized with any temporary dizziness in the head – an epidemic which prevailed among the electors, during the contest, to a most alarming extent, and under the influence of which they might frequently be seen lying on the pavements in a state of utter insensibility.

Dickens C *Pickwick Papers* Penguin Classics edn, 1986, pp 240–41, 255

D   *This extract is taken from a Royal Commission Report by J Mitchell on electioneering abuses at Sudbury, 1840.*

... This is a borough to which it is notorious that for a long period of time gentlemen of property have brought their money for the purpose of presenting to the poverty of the voters temptations which it was calculated they would be unable to withstand, and thereby they would be induced to give their suffrages ...

It is obvious that the gentlemen who bring their money into the town for the purpose of influencing the suffrages, and the gentlemen residing in the town who become their committee men, inflict the most cruel injury on the unhappy voters. Their habits of industry are seriously broken in upon; their health suffers from the unwonted hospitality; their principles of manly fair-dealing are corrupted by the application of an irresistible sum of money from one side, and then by the irresistible counteraction of a still larger sum from the other; and worst of all, their peace of mind and their reliance on their Almighty Father are ruined by open, daring perjury, which destroys their sense of moral obligation in this world, and awfully endangers their salvation in the next.

Report of the Assistant Hand-Loom Commissioners
1840 *Parliamentary Papers 1842*, Vol. VII, pp 943–5

Questions

1 Which items in Source A do you think were justifiable and which would you criticise? Overall what does the source show about the conduct of the election?
2 What are the values and what are the dangers of using literary sources like Source C in writing history?
3 To what extent does the Commissioner's report in Source D suggest that Dickens' account was historically accurate?
4 How far do Sources B, C and D together suggest that elections after the first Reform Act were similar to an election in 1830 as shown in Source A?

5 What further types of evidence would you require to assess the extent of corruption after 1832?

Notes

1 Spring vans – vans with springs which most carts did not have

1.3 The Second Reform Act – A Product of Popular Pressure or Parliamentary Manoeuvre?

The second Reform Act of 1867 nearly doubled the British electorate, and there has been fierce historical controversy over why such a wide-ranging measure was passed and why a Conservative government initiated it?

Some have seen the measure as a response to increasing public pressure in general and to the dangers demonstrated by Reform meetings in Hyde Park in particular. Much attention has been given to disturbances at the park in July 1866 when a length of railings was pushed down. Royden Harrison[1] argued that a later meeting in Hyde Park on 6 May 1867 did much to persuade MPs to accept radical amendments during the following month. Others such as Maurice Cowling[2] and Lord Blake[3] have explained the Act more in terms of parliamentary manoeuvres – the Conservative government's calculations of tactical party advantage and the political ambitions of Benjamin Disraeli who masterminded its passage through the House of Commons.

A   *A diary entry from the Conservative minister Sir Stafford Northcote recording a meeting with Disraeli to discuss the formation of a new government, 29 June 1866.*

Dis[raeli] thought we should gain little by addressing ourselves to the Adullamites in the

H[ouse] ... Lowe's appointment would be rather too much of a challenge to the Reform party, and would look like the decided adoption of an anti-Reform policy, ''while after all perhaps we may be the men to settle the question''.
British Museum Additional Manuscripts 50063 A f.93

B *'The Times' reports disturbances at Hyde Park, July 1866.*

... a number of the lowest rabble of the metropolis assembled in the park near the Marble Arch ... They wreaked their vengeance on the flowers and shrubs by wantonly plucking them up by the roots. The attention of the police does not appear to have been directed to what was going on until about 1 o'clock ... It soon appeared that the mob, though entirely without leaders or organization, were able to resist the police with a certain amount of success. Petty conflicts took place during the whole of the afternoon, though in no instance, as far as could be ascertained, were the injuries sustained on either side serious ... Nothing at all approaching to a general engagement between the police and the ''people'' took place during the evening, but slight scuffles occurred every few minutes ... These partial disturbances continued till half-past 8 o'clock, when the police, aided by the military, mustered all their strength, and in a short time succeeded in clearing the park ...

The Times, 25 July 1866

C *A letter from the Prime Minister, Lord Derby, to Disraeli, 16 September 1866.*

... I am coming reluctantly to the conclusion that we shall have to deal with the question of Reform ... if we should be beaten on some great leading principle, we should have a definite issue on which to go to the country ...

In: Monypenny WF; Buckle GE, 1916, *The Life of Benjamin Disraeli, Earl of Beaconsfield,* Vol. IV, John Murray, p 453

D *'The Times' reports the Hyde Park meeting of 6 May 1867.*

This great meeting, the threat of holding which in defiance of the Government, and still more the Government preparations to prevent its being held, have kept the metropolis in a state of chronic alarm and agitation for the last month, was held yesterday evening, and passed off with the quietness and good order of a temperance meeting. Of course, in the face of such a happy result, it will be very easy to assert, now that all has gone off smoothly and well, that no other course was ever intended, and that the authorities never meant either to forbid the meeting or prevent it. It is somewhat too late in the day, however, now, when the military and police precautions adopted or intended to be adopted to suppress the meeting are known, to announce that it was never contemplated to prevent it ...

Of the meeting or demonstration, or whatever the League may choose to call it, it is really difficult to say much. It was a vast assemblage of people, certainly not less than 40,000 to 50,000 people being in the park. Of these, however, probably not much more than a tenth were what we may call the Reformers ...

The Times, 7 May 1867

E *Another report of the Hyde Park meeting, 6 May 1867, in a Liberal newspaper 'The Daily News'.*

The numbers present in the park have been variously estimated at from 100,000 to 150,000, and probably the last mentioned figure would be nearer the truth ...

The Daily News, 7 May 1867

F *A letter from Disraeli to a Conservative Minister, Gathorne Hardy, in which he explains why he accepted an amendment from the radical Hodgkinson.*

I waited until the question was put, when, having revolved everything in my mind, I felt that the critical moment had arrived, and when, without in the slightest degree receding from our principle and position of a rating and residential franchise, we might take a step which would destroy the present agitation and extinguish Gladstone and Co. I therefore accepted the spirit of H's amendment.

> In: Buckle G E 1916 *The Life of Benjamin Disraeli,*
> *Earl of Beaconsfield*, Vol. IV, John Murray, p 540

G *A Conservative MP, Mr Henley, speaking on the Committee Stage of the Reform Bill, 20 May 1867.*

... Meetings were held in different places all over the country in which no mere reduction of the franchise was talked about, but in which manhood suffrage was insisted upon. That was the state of things we had to meet last session – and what happened then? Why, a Bill was brought in, not merely reducing the figure, but doing away with all payment of rates. How was that Bill received? Meetings were held throughout the country, but did they assent to it? Far from it ... The opinion universally expressed at those meetings was that they would accept it – how? – as an instalment ... I believe the only mode, and therefore the Conservative mode, of stopping that which these public meetings have asked for is to take in all those who pay their share of the burdens of the State and let them have the privileges of citizenship. I will not go further into what have been the causes of the position in which we are placed; but I believe that if you had attempted to stand still the question would have gone on from agitation to agitation until it had introduced into the country a state of things which all of us would be sorry to see. I believe the ground that has been taken is the true Conservative ground; and for this reason – that it is the old ground of the Constitution ...

> *Hansard*, 20 May 1867. Ser. 3, Vol. 187: 801–2

Questions

1 What do you understand by
  a 'the Adullamites' (Source A line 2)?
  b 'the quietness and good order of a temperance meeting' (Source D lines 7–8)?
  c a Bill 'not merely reducing the figure, but doing away with all payment of rates' (Source G lines 7–9)?
2 What do Sources B, D and E suggest was the significance of
  a the Hyde Park disturbances in July 1866?
  b the Hyde Park meeting on 6 May 1867?
3 Look carefully at the dating both of Sources A, C and F and the events at Hyde Park. How far do these sources suggest that the events at the park and other popular agitation influenced government policy?
4 On what grounds did Mr Henley suggest that the Reform Bill was a Conservative measure in Source G?
5 For what other reasons did Conservative MPs support a radical reform bill?[4]

Notes

1 Harrison R 1965 'The tenth April of Spencer Walpole: The problem of revolution in relation to reform, 1865–67.' In: *Before the Socialists* Routledge and Kegan Paul
2 Cowling M 1967 *1867: Disraeli, Gladstone and Revolution* Cambridge University Press
3 Blake R 1966 *Disraeli* Eyre and Spottiswoode
4 For further summary of historians' views on why such a major reform was passed see:
Wright D G 1970 *Democracy and Reform 1815–1885* Longman
Walton J K 1987 *The Second Reform Act* Methuen

1.4 Politicians and their Supporters – Political Clubs in the Late Nineteenth Century

The great growth in the electorate under the second Reform Act encouraged the political parties to develop local organisations and to recruit working class members. This is seen at a national level in the National Union of Conservative Associations of 1867 and the National Liberal Federation established in 1877. It is more difficult to trace at a local level where much of the available evidence comes from newspapers.[1]

A *A report in the 'Salford Weekly News' of a meeting of the Broughton branch of the Salford Liberal Association in Lancashire.*

Mr THOMAS SMITH presided, and briefly addressed the meeting, congratulating the members upon the fact that they could now hold their meetings upon their own premises. The SECRETARY read a report, from which it appeared that the rooms in Cumberland Street had been purchased, and that the deeds were being prepared ... it was further intended, if the funds were forthcoming, to erect a commodious billiard room, which should be replete with every convenience, and contain a full-sized table. This, combined with a reading room, smoke room, chess, draughts, a good supply of papers and periodicals, and the opportunity for obtaining tea, coffee, cigars etc., at fixed charges on the premises, would, it was confidently hoped, offer such advantages as should induce all Liberals of the district to enrol themselves as members ...

Salford Weekly News, 17 February 1872

B Salford Constitutional Association Annual Pic-Nic and Sports

The annual *fete* of the Salford Constitutional Association, took place at Lyme Park, Disley, on Saturday afternoon, and was a decided success. The weather was delightfully fine, and nothing could have been more enjoyable – especially to those residing in a populous town like Salford – than to breathe the fresh air and admire the picturesque scenery of this charming spot. The members of the Association and their friends, numbering altogether about 2,000 ... left Ordsall Lane station by two special trains ... At five o'clock the racing sports commenced ...

After the last deciding heat had been run, the party assembled near the refreshment tent, and the prizes to the successful competitors were distributed ... Prior to the distribution the new 'Conservative Gallop', composed by Mr J A Gifford, the bandmaster of the Salford Volunteers ... was played (for the first time publicly) by the band ...

Salford Weekly Chronicle, 2 August 1873

C Salford Liberal Association Annual Picnic

The annual picnic of the members and friends of the Salford Liberal Association was held on Saturday last, at Chatsworth, the seat of his Grace the Duke of Devonshire. The party were conveyed by two trains ...

The CHAIRMAN said he trusted that those annual picnics would only have one effect upon them as workers in the Liberal cause – namely, that they would be cemented more closely together, and that they would be attached more firmly to their principles ... They must not, however, allow the association to exist simply for recreation, either on occasions like that or in the wards. Their clubs, also, must not be used merely as places of recreation, but must be utilised for their banding together for the work they had to do. He hoped this would be remembered in the time coming, especially as they had before them in all probability a re-election of their parliamentary representatives.

Salford Weekly News, 10 August 1878

D   *From a Report of the Annual Meeting of Brigg Conservative Association in Lincolnshire.*

Mr WINN M.P. ... said he was there to take part in the organisation of the Brigg Conservative Association. He was delighted to find that Brigg had taken the lead in forming an association of that kind within its own polling district, and he had every reason to believe that within a short period similar associations would be formed in all the other polling districts in North Lincolnshire, and, if that were done, he did not fear the result of any future election, come when the election might ...

The Lincoln, Rutland and Stamford Mercury,
9 December 1881

E   **Pendleton Liberal Club**
The President Entertains the Members

On the invitation of the new President (Councillor Russell) the members of this club sat down to a substantial tea on Tuesday night ...
   Councillor Hewitt ... regretted – if he might be allowed to say so – that the social advantages of the club were not made a little more subservient to the political advantages. That and all other political clubs had fallen short in the objects for which they were established, the political features having been made subservient to social considerations; in fact, social matters had rather leavened the whole lump. He wished that circumstance was a little more clear to the members, for was it not their duty as members to do something to promote the success of Liberalism in the district? ...
   An entertainment followed ...

Pendleton, Salford and Broughton Reporter, 20 April
1889

Questions

1 What similarities do these sources suggest between popular organisations on the Liberal and Conservative sides?

2 In what ways do they indicate that club facilities and social activities could help or hinder political work in the two parties?
3 What is the value of reports such as these in understanding late nineteenth-century politics? What other evidence do you need to assess the importance of local party organisations?
4 Why did people join later nineteenth-century political parties? How important were social factors and what other reasons led people to join political clubs and associations? How were these reasons likely to differ between the Liberal and Conservative parties?[2]

Notes

1 Much of the evidence in this section is cited in:
   Garrard J 1977 'Parties, members and voters after 1867: A local study.' *Historical Journal.* Revised version printed in: Gourvish T R, O'Day A (eds) 1988 *Later Victorian Britain 1867–1900* Macmillan
2 For more information see:
   Vincent J 1972 *The Formation of the British Liberal Party 1857–68* Pelican
   Blake R 1985 *The Conservative Party from Peel to Thatcher* Fontana

1.5 Votes for Women – The Early Twentieth-Century Controversy

The struggle for women's votes is normally associated with the suffragettes – the Women's Social and Political Union or WSPU – founded in 1903. In fact there was lively debate over women's rights in the late nineteenth century; the suffragettes were only one of a number of campaigning organisations and the effects of their militancy are debatable. But the controversy over women's suffrage undoubtedly reached its height with suffragette activity in the early twentieth century, and Mrs

Pankhurst (the WSPU leader) and Lord Curzon (the Conservative peer and future Foreign Secretary) were two of its leading protagonists. What conflicting claims did they make and how did they support their arguments?

A *This extract is taken from a lecture on 'The Importance of the Vote' given at Portman Rooms, 24 March 1908 by Mrs Pankhurst.*

... it is important that women should have the vote in order that in the government of the country the women's point of view should be put forward ... Very little has been done by legislation for women for many years – for obvious reasons. More and more of the time of members of Parliament is occupied by the claims which are made on behalf of the people who are organised in various ways in order to promote the interests of their industrial organisations or their political or social organisations ... [An MP's] time is fully taken up by attending to the needs of the people who have sent him to Parliament ... you cannot take up a newspaper, you cannot go to a conference, you cannot even go to church, without hearing a great deal of talk about social reform and a demand for social legislation. Of course, it is obvious that that kind of legislation – and the Liberal Government tell us that if they remain in office long enough we are going to have a great deal of it – is of vital importance to women ... We are hearing about legislation to decide what kind of homes people are to live in. That surely is a question for women. Surely every woman, when she seriously thinks about it, will wonder how men by themselves can have the audacity to think that they can say what homes ought to be without consulting women. Then take education. Since 1870 men have been trying to find out how to educate children. I think they have not yet realised that if they are ever to find out how to educate children, they will have to take women into their confidence ...

... I assure you that no woman who enters into this agitation need feel that she has got to give up a single one of her woman's duties in the home. She learns to feel that she is attaching a larger meaning to those duties which have been woman's duties since the race began, and will be till the race has ceased to be ... The home is the home of everybody of the nation. No nation can have a proper home unless women as well as men give their best to its building up and to making it what a home ought to be, a place where every single child born into it shall have a fair chance of growing up to be a fit, and a happy, and a useful member of the community.

B *Lord Curzon argues against women's suffrage in a speech at Glasgow in 1912.*

The whole life of the working man is a political school. The papers which he reads every day, the public meetings which he attends, the debating societies to which many belong, the enormous influence of the Press – all of these are a mechanism for familiarizing the working man with his duties ... it is a different question when you come to women. Shall we be wise if to this uncertain element in the existing electorate we add the enormous and incalculable factor of a preponderant vote of women? They, too, are necessarily devoid of the requisite experience and training, but the difference is greater than that. The conditions of their education, the physiological functions they have to perform, the duties of their lives render it impossible, with due regard to the interests of their sex, to acquire the training and experience of which I am speaking. And such an addition cannot be the casual addition of a few hundreds, or thousands, or a few millions. It must mean in the long run – and probably in the short run – the addition of a number of women to the register which would place them in numerical command. ...

Now you may ask, what would be the effect on the government of the State and the Empire if a majority of women had the vote. Let me try to answer. I grant you there might very easily be issues in our life upon which the votes of women would have immaterial consequences, some upon which the consequences might even be beneficial. But those cases do not cover the whole of the political field. Issues sometimes arise in public affairs – you can see them on the horizon now – great issues of peace and war, of treaties and alliances, of the treatment to be adopted towards our Colonies and dependencies. An unwise, and still more an emotional, decision of those issues might in circumstances which it is easy to imagine lead to the disruption and even to the ruin of the Empire ... Suppose that it was a question of instituting national compulsory military training in this country. I ask you, are those the sort of questions that in a reflective mood you would wish to be decided by a majority of women? And take the final and crucial test of all; take the test of war. Supposing this country were threatened with war and an election were being fought upon the steps that ought to be taken in the supreme crisis of our national fortune, would you like your destinies at such a moment to be decided by women? ...

What is the good of talking about the equality of the sexes? The first whiz of the bullet, the first boom of the cannon, and where is the equality of the sexes? When it comes to fighting, war has to be decided, always has been decided, and always will be decided, by one sex alone.

In: Chapman-Huston D M (ed.) 1915 *Subjects of the Day: Selection of Speeches and Writings by Earl Curzon of Kedleston* George Allen and Unwin, pp 301–4

C   *Poster supporting women's suffrage.*

D   *An anti-suffrage poster, 1912.*

Questions

1 How can the scene in Source D be used as an argument against women voting?

2 How effectively do Mrs Pankhurst's arguments in Source A counter this view?

3 a Which occupations and offices does Source C show that women could already hold before World War I?

  b What argument is the poster making?

4 How effectively do Lord Curzon's arguments in Source B counter the opinions portrayed in Source C?

5 a What social reforms did Liberal governments introduce in 1906–14 on which women should have been consulted according to Mrs Pankhurst's arguments?

  b What imperial, diplomatic and defensive problems did Britain face in 1912 on which women would not be competent to make decisions according to Lord Curzon's arguments?[1]

Notes

1 Refer to text or topic books covering the period; eg
Read D 1979 *England 1868–1914* Longman, Chaps. 28–30
Feuchtwanger E J 1985 *Democracy and Empire* Edward Arnold, Chaps. 8, 9
Aikin, K W W 1972 *The Last Years of Liberal England 1900–1914* Collins

Opposite: A Suffragette's Home National League for Opposing Woman Suffrage

2 The Industrial Revolution and Social Change

2.1 The Working Class Standard of Living in the Industrial Revolution

There has probably been more bitter and long-lasting controversy between historians over the question of working class living standards in the late eighteenth and early nineteenth centuries than over any other issue in the period.

On one side, historians labelled 'optimists' broadly, and sometimes confidently, assert that standards rose. On the other side, 'pessimists' deny this just as strongly. The disagreement is partly because of inadequate information and difficulties in defining what we mean by living standards, but the debate is also fuelled by political differences. Right-wing supporters of capitalism generally wish to believe that the masses benefited from industrialisation; left wingers, often influenced by Marx's analysis of working class immiseration during the Industrial Revolution, more often wish to perceive a decline.

Source A represents one of the most useful recent attempts to calculate real wages (ie, workers' wages in relation to the prices of goods they purchased), but it is an uncertain indicator of the national position[1]. First there are problems in finding and selecting wage rates from a representative series of occupations. Then there are difficulties in weighting a cost-of-living index; ie, deciding how much an average working class family spent on different items and what allowance should therefore be made for various prices when calculating living costs. Often the prices available are wholesale ones and not the retail prices which workers actually paid when they bought the goods in streets or shops. Unlike some estimates, Lindert and Williamson's calculations shown in Source A include an allowance for rent, but it is based on only a few dozen cottages in Staffordshire. In addition we have to remember that there were regional variations in wages, prices and patterns of consumption which we cannot know precisely, and for which we cannot make exact allowance. In addition, there is the problem of deciding which years to choose when making comparisons, as the relationship between wages and prices altered markedly according to short-term economic fluctuations and harvest conditions.

It should also be stressed that while most real-wage series show a marked improvement in the course of the early nineteenth century on which this section concentrates, there is more doubt about the late eighteenth century. A study of London building workers' living standards has suggested a marked decline[2], while research in north Staffordshire suggests an optimistic impression for the period in the industrial Midlands and North[3]. This section can only suggest the sort of evidence and types of problems encountered in assessing living standards at the start of the 1815–1914 period.

A *The graph shows adult male average full-time earnings for selected groups of workers, 1755–1851, at constant prices.*

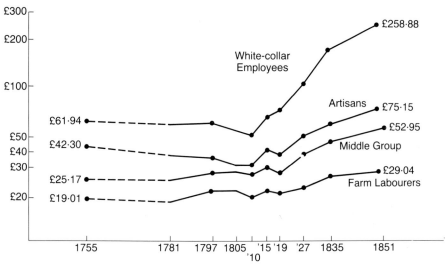

Lindert P H, Williamson J G 'English workers' living standards during the Industrial Revolution: A new look'.
Economic History Review, February 1983, p 12

B *Discipline in a Leeds linen mill, 1821.*

The hands had very particular printed instructions set before them which are as particularly attended to ... so strict are the instructions that if an overseer of a room be found talking to any person in the mill during working hours he is dismissed immediately ... everyone, manager, overseers, mechanics, oilers, spreaders, spinners and reelers, have their particular duty pointed out to them, and if they transgress, they are instantly turned off as unfit for their situation.

Brown W 'Information regarding flax spinning at Leeds, 1821,' 1960. In: Rimmer W G *Marshalls of Leeds, Flax Spinners 1788–1886* Cambridge University Press, p 119

C *Unemployment in the Lancashire textile town of Bolton during the slump year of 1842.*

Trade	Total employed in 1836	Total employed whole or part-time in 1842	Percentage unemployed
Mills	8,124	3,063 (full time)	60
Ironworkers	2,110	1,325 (short time)	36
Carpenters	150	24	84
Bricklayers	120	16	87
Stonemasons	150	50	66
Tailors	500	250	50
Shoemakers	80	40	50

Hobsbawm E J 1957 'The British standard of living 1790–1850.' *Economic History Review*. Compiled from: Ashworth H 1842 'Statistics of the present depression of trade in Bolton.' *J. Statistical Society*, Vol. 5, p 74

D *Examples of foodstuffs which were sometimes adulterated with other substances to add weight and bulk, from a medical investigation, 1851–54.*

BREAD—Mashed Potatoes, Water
BUTTER—Water
COFFEE—Chicory, roasted Wheat, Rye and Potato Flours, Burnt Beans, Acorns, Mangel-wurzel
SUGAR—Potato Flour, Tapioca Starch
TEA—Exhausted Tea Leaves; Leaves other than those of Tea, foreign and native; amongst the latter those of Sycamore, Horse Chestnut and Plum; Lie Tea; Paddy Husk

> Hassall A H 1855 *Food and its Adulterations;* Comprising the Reports of the Analytical Sanitary Commission of *The Lancet* 1851-1854, Introduction
> p iv

Questions

1 Summarise the changes in real wages between 1781 and 1851 shown in Source A.
2 In what ways do Sources B, C and D suggest that these may not give an adequate indication of changes in living standards?
3 Were the problems and hardships indicated in Sources B, C and D novel in the Industrial Revolution period? If not, how far were they likely to have increased in intensity? How far do you think these sources are representative of a national situation?
4 Families moved voluntarily into the expanding towns and factories of industrial England in the nineteenth century. Consider how far this can be taken as an indicator that they offered better conditions of life.

Notes

1 On problems involved in real-wage calculations see:
Flinn M W 'Trends in real wages 1750–1850.' *Economic History Review*, August 1974
Lindert P H, Williamson J G 'English workers' living standards during the Industrial Revolution: A new look.' *Economic History Review*, February 1983.
Comments by Flinn, Lindert and Williamson, *Economic History Review*, February 1984.
Crafts N F R 1985 *British Economic Growth during the Industrial Revolution* Oxford University Press, Chap. 5
2 Schwarz L D, 'The standard of living in the long run: London 1700–1860.' *Economic History Review*, February 1985
Hunt E H, Botham F W, 'Wages in Britain during the Industrial Revolution.' *Economic History Review*, August 1987
3 There is a summary of the debate up to the mid-1980s from a pessimist perspective in:
Rule J 1986 *The Labouring Classes in Early Industrial England, 1750–1850* Longman, Part 1
For a shorter summary see:
Royle E 1987, *Modern Britain, a Social History 1750–1985* Edward Arnold, Chap. 4
May T 1987 *An Economic and Social History of Britain, 1760–1970* Longman, Chap. 2

2.2 The Birth of Class Consciousness?

Eighteenth-century men normally described their society in terms of ranks or orders: nineteenth-century commentators spoke of classes. In the early nineteenth century, so it is argued, class consciousness was born. How classes should be defined, whether there were two, three or five classes, or indeed what class consciousness means at all, are all subjects of anguished dispute among historians and sociologists. It is generally agreed that class consciousness involves some identification with others in a similar economic and social position on a nationwide basis and a clear sense of conflicting interests between classes. Whether such class consciousness was the experience of a small minority or of the masses, whether it was a permanent and maturing state of mind or more a temporary response to economic adversity and how far it was sufficiently strong to predominate over more traditional loyalties based on trades or localities are all debatable issues. But there was, no doubt, an awakening of some class feeling: how was it born?

A *From an analysis of society and public opinion in the 1820s.*

...Where freedom and civilization exist, wealth is so entirely the only power either to individuals or to government, that no other means or choice is left of distinguishing the several classes of society, than by the property of the individuals of which they are formed.

Mackinnon W A 1828 *On the Rise, Progress and Present State of Public Opinion in Great Britain and Other Parts of the World* Saunders and Ottey, p 2

B *A poem in 'The Poor Man's Guardian'.*

ON WAGES
Wages should form the price of goods;
Yes, wages should be all,
Then we who work to make the goods,
Should *justly have them all*;
But if their price be made of rent,
Tithes, taxes, profits all,
Then we who work to make the goods,
Shall have – just none at all.
ONE OF THE KNOW-NOTHINGS.

The Poor Man's Guardian, 7 January 1832. In Hollis P 1973 *Class and Conflict in Nineteenth-Century England 1815–1850* Routledge and Kegan Paul, p 50

C *From a letter from the political philosopher, James Mill, to the Lord Chancellor, Lord Brougham, 3 September 1832.*

I should have little fear of the propagation among the common people of any doctrines hostile to property ... But there are ... at present, aids of that propagation, which may operate deplorably ... [one is] the illicit, cheap publications, in which the doctrine of the right of the labouring people, who they say are the only producers, to all that is produced, is very generally preached. The alarming nature of this evil you will understand when I inform you that these publications are superseding the Sunday newspapers, and every other channel through which the people might get better information ...

Bain A 1882 *James Mill* Longman, p 365

D *From the Chartist newspaper 'The Northern Star'.*

... The attention of the labouring classes – the real 'people' – has been successively (and yet, to a certain degree, simultaneously) aroused by the injuries they have sustained by the operation of a corrupt system of patronage hanging round their necks a host of locusts, in the shape of idle and useless pensioners, and a swarm of hornets, in the form of mischievous placemen and Commissioners, to support whom they are weighed to the earth by the pressure of taxation; by the operation of the Corn Laws, which made rents high, and bread dear; by the iniquitous protection of the fundholders, which made money dear and labour cheap; by the horrors of the Factory System, which immolates their progeny, and coins the blood of their children into gold, for 'merciless griping ruffians;' and, by the abominations of the Poor Law Act, which virtually and practically denies them the right to live. All these, and a hundred minor grievances, subservient to the same grand end, (of making the working classes beasts of burden – hewers of wood, and drawers of water – to the Aristocracy, Jewocracy, Millocracy, Shopocracy, and every other Ocracy that feeds on human vitals,) have roused the feelings of the people and prompted the respective parties to seek a remedy for the smarting of their wounds ... all these horrible effects sprung from one fearful cause. The laws, being made *for* and not *by* the people, took no cognizance of their interests, but considered only how they might be made promotive of the interests of the law makers ...

The Northern Star, 4 August 1838

E   *A Manchester clergyman, Canon Parkinson, describes his expanding industrial city.*

There is no town in the world where the distance between the rich and the poor is so great, or the barrier between them so difficult to be crossed. I once ventured to designate the town of Manchester the most *aristocratic* town in England; and, in the sense in which the term was used, the expression is not hyperbolical. The separation between the different classes, and the consequent ignorance of each other's habits and condition, are far more complete in this place than in any country of the older nations of Europe, or the agricultural parts of our own kingdom. There is far less *personal* communication between the master cotton spinner and his workmen, between the calico printer and his blue-handed boys, between the master tailor and his apprentices, than there is between the Duke of Wellington and the humblest labourer on his estate, or than there *was* between good old George the Third and the meanest errand-boy about his palace. I mention this not as a matter of blame, but I state it simply as a *fact*.

> Parkinson R 'On the present condition of the labouring poor in Manchester, 1841.' In: Briggs A 1968 *Victorian Cities* p 114

Questions

1 What do you understand by
   a 'pensioners' (Source D line 7)?
   b 'placemen' (Source D line 9)?
   c 'fundholders' (Source D line 14)?
2 What economic, political and social reasons do these sources suggest for the development of class consciousness?
3 a Which of the sources were apparently written by middle class and which by working class people? Explain your answer.
   b Which of the sources indicate class hostility and how do they show this?
4 What are the advantages and disadvantages of each of these sources as indicators of the extent of class consciousness?
5 a What 'illicit, cheap publications' spread 'doctrines hostile to property' (Source C lines 5–6 and 2–3) in the 1830s?[1]
   b Which laws, in addition to the Corn Laws and the Poor Law Act, could be considered 'promotive of the interests of the law makers' in 1838 (Source D final lines)?[2]
6 What further evidence would you consider necessary to prove the existence of class consciousness and how far do you think this is available?[3]

Notes

1 See text and topic books, for example,
   Briggs A 1959 *The Age of Improvement* Longman, Chap. 6
   Royle E 1971 *Radical Politics 1790–1900 Religion and Unbelief* Longman, Chap. 3
   Royle E 1986 *Chartism* Longman, 2nd edn, Chap. 2
   Dinwiddy J R 1986 *From Luddism to the First Reform Bill* Blackwell, Chaps. 3, 4
   Wright D G 1988 *Popular Radicalism* Longman, Chap. 5
2 See text books, for example,
   Briggs A 1959 *The Age of Improvement* Longman
   Gash N 1979 *Aristocracy and People* Edward Arnold
3 For summaries of the historical debate on class see:
   Morris R J 1979 *Class and Class Consciousness in the Industrial Revolution 1780–1850* Macmillan
   Rule J 1986 *The Labouring Classes in Early Industrial England 1750–1850* Longman, Conclusion
   Wright D G 1988 *Popular Radicalism* Longman, Chap. 1

2.3 Railways – 'A Device for Making the World Smaller'

A British railway system developed in the mid-nineteenth century following the pioneering success of the Liverpool–Manchester line which opened in 1830. Britain had over 5000 miles of railway by 1850, over 11 000 by 1865 and over 18 000 by 1900. Modern statistical studies suggest that contemporaries often exaggerated the mid-nineteenth century effects of the railways and that the rail network only made its major impact on the economy, society and urban geography of Britain in the later years of the century. However, for many people the coming of the 'iron road' was revolutionary. How did the increased mobility affect the Victorian way of life?

A *From a Lancashire newspaper, 1844.*

... the poor man's life is passed in one dull, unchequered, unvaried course. He has no pastimes, no diversions; he is confined from year's end to year's end in some squalid, uncomfortable dwelling, and seldom leaves the precincts of his pent up alley to wander forth in green fields, fresh air, and pleasant places. The treat, therefore, which was provided for the poor of this town, in the way of a pleasure excursion by railway to Fleetwood, on Monday last, under the auspices of the Preston Temperance Excursion Committee, was truly a novel and delightful feature in their existence – a bright and cheering spot in the dreary desert of their pilgrimage.

The Preston Chronicle and Lancashire Advertiser,
17 August 1844

B *William Johnston describes the state of England in 1851.*

The most important event of the last quarter of a century in English history is the establish-ment of Railroads. The stupendous magnitude of the capital they have absorbed – the changes they have produced in the habits of society ... above all, the new and excessive activities to which they have given rise – must lead all who reflect upon the subject to admit that the importance of the general result of these great undertakings can scarcely be exaggerated. They have done much towards changing the old deliberate and thoughtful habits of Englishmen. People who breakfast in York and dine in London – who may be summoned from Liverpool to the metropolis in three or four minutes by electric telegraph, and answer the summons in person within six or seven hours by the express train – acquire a habit of pressure and velocity in all they do ... The railway has made Manchester, as it were, a part of London, and infected London with the sentiments of Manchester. Even the court catches the spirit of trade.

Johnston W 1851 *England As It Is*, Vol. 1,
John Murray, pp 260, 262

C *The arrival of a workmen's train at Victoria Station, 1865.*

D *A Victorian statistician, R Dudley Baxter, assesses the effects of railways by 1865.*

... Increased facilities of transit led to increased trade; increased trade gave greater employment, and improved wages; the diminution in the cost of transit and the repeal of fiscal duties cheapened provisions; and the immense flood of commerce which set in since 1850 has raised the incomes and the prosperity of the working classes to an unprecedented height. Railways were the first cause of this great change ... How did the country population attain their present prosperity? Simply by the emigration to the towns or colonies of the redundant labourers. This emigration was scarcely possible till the construction of railways. Up to that time the farm labourer was unable to migrate; from that time he became a migratory animal. The increase of population in agricultural counties stopped, or was changed into a decrease, and the labourers ceased to be too numerous for the work. To this cause is principally owing the sufficiency of employment and wages throughout the agricultural portion of the kingdom.

Baxter R D 1866 'Railway extension and its results.' *J. Statistical Society*, Vol. XXIX, p 567. In: Carus-Wilson E M (ed) 1962 *Essays in Economic History*, Vol. III, Edward Arnold, pp 43–4

E *Samuel Smiles comments on the impact of railways by the 1870s.*

One of the remarkable effects of railways has been to extend the residential area of all large towns and cities. This is especially notable in the case of London ...

The improved state of the communications of the City with the country has had a marked effect upon its population. While the action of the railways has been to add largely to the number of persons living in London, it has also been accompanied by their dispersion over a much larger area. Thus the population of the central parts of London is constantly decreasing, whereas that of the suburban districts is as constantly increasing ...

> Smiles S 1874 *Lives of the Engineers, The Locomotive: George and Robert Stephenson*, Introduction, pp xix–xx

Questions

1 What benefits do these sources show that the railway brought for
   a the middle class?
   b the working class?
2 What types of workers were using the train in Source C and how can you identify them?
3 Which writer suggests a disadvantage of speedier railway travel and what is it?
4 What indications are there of excitement or enthusiasm over the railways in Sources A, B, D and E, and how does this affect the way in which an historian should use the sources?
5 Several mid-nineteenth century commentators claimed that the working class benefited from the railways more than any other part of society. How far do you agree?[1]

Notes

1 See:
Read D 1979 *England 1868–1914* Longman, Chap. 4
Royle E 1987 *Modern Britain; A Social History 1750–1985* Edward Arnold, Chap. 1
May T 1987 *An Economic and Social History of Britain, 1760–1970* Longman, Chap. 6

3 Working Class Responses 1815–50

3.1 Rural Experience: The 1830 Agricultural Labourers' Revolt

English rural life was punctuated by unrest in the early nineteenth century – surreptiously through rick-burning or cattle maiming and sometimes publicly through demonstration and violence. By far the most serious outbreaks spread from Kent across southern and eastern England in the autumn and winter of 1830–31. Secretly, protestors committed arson and wrote threatening letters: openly, villagers joined together in large bands which presented demands for higher wages and frequently broke the threshing machines which deprived men of winter employment. Why did the revolt take place and what did it show about the way rural society was developing?

example in the records of English privation. His weekly wages will not at this moment buy him much more than half the quantity of corn which, in the cottage of his grandfather, was the consumption of the week. With the positive increase of wealth and poverty, not only has been widened the distance between the two extremes of society, but the sympathy between all who possess *something*, and all who possess no property but their labour, has sensibly and mournfully diminished. Instead of being fairly fused and incorporated, the people of this United Kingdom may now be said to lie in strata one above the other, and the pressure of the superincumbent masses on the lowest has become altogether intolerable ...

...The farmer *is* now, or pretends to be, a gentleman. The farming servant *is* a miserable outcast from the farmer's dwelling – an ill-paid, half-starved, heartless, and exasperated slave.

The Times, 30 October 1830

A *'The Times' comments on the start of the disturbances in Kent.*

The tendencies of the national condition for the last half century have been, to make the rich man richer, and the poor man miserably poorer, than at any well-authenticated period of our modern history. The rich man of the present day can command a much greater amount of the marketable goods of life than his predecessor of fifty years back; and rich men, besides, have become more numerous than formerly. The humble labourer, on the other hand, has experienced a fall of wages, and a progressive loss of comforts, without

B *A letter in 'The Times'. (The paper claimed to have the name and address of the writer.)*

... I was present at a lecture delivered at East Bourne, in Sussex, by Mr Cobbett. In that lecture he told his hearers (who were principally labouring men), that a revolution must inevitably take place in this country; 'and,' says this dangerous man, 'it must be worked by such men as I see before me' ... Up to that time no appearance of disorder had taken place, and the farmers were still free from the ravages of these monsters. But mark the sequel! In Battel the conflagrations have since been nightly, and East Bourne is now the scene of destruction. That there are active agents abroad exciting and assisting the people to the fulfilment of these prophecies, there can be no doubt . . .

I am, Sir, your obedient servant,
AN ENGLISHMAN

The Times, 13 November 1830

C *Report in 'The Times' from a correspondent at Hastings, Sussex.*

Divested of its objectionable character, as a dangerous precedent, the conduct of the peasantry has been admirable. There is no ground for concluding that there has been any extensive concert amongst them. Each parish, generally speaking, has risen *per se*[1]; in many places their proceedings have been managed with astonishing coolness and regularity . . . The farmers have notice to meet the men; a deputation of two or three of the latter produce a written statement, well drawn up, which the farmers are required to sign; the spokesman, sometimes a Dissenting or Methodist teacher, fulfils his office with great propriety and temper . . .

The Times, 17 November 1830

D *Letter to the Home Secretary from the magistrates of the Andover division of Hampshire, 20 November 1830.*

. . . numerous Assemblies of the labouring classes have taken place in this Neighbourhood.

The object of these meetings is to demand in a clamorous manner an increase of wages. The destruction of all threshing-Machines and to require of the proprietors of Land and Tythes a reduction of Rents and Composition.

The practice seems to be to form local combinations between contiguous Parishes to force all reluctant persons into their Schemes and to threaten a unison of Forces for the accomplishment of their purposes. They also demand and levy contributions in Goods and Money from the persons whose habitations they visit.

PRO Home Office Papers 52/7

E *From a report on how 'to discover an incendiary in the country' sent by the managing director of the County Fire Office, London to the Police Officer, 24 December 1830.*

If the spot be close by a public way, on which strangers as well as the neighbours and family are accustomed to pass, your inquiries can no longer be limited to the neighbourhood: but the stories about strangers in gigs, and about fire-balls, have in no instance been realized; in many instances they have been invented by persons living near the spot, who are themselves the incendiaries. In almost every instance, wherein conviction has taken place, the culprit has been a servant of the sufferer, or a person living near to him, acting under some motive of revenge. One or two political enthusiasts have gone about in gigs, or on horseback, disseminating seditious speeches and papers, but no materials for firing have been found on them.

PRO Home Office Papers 40/25, p 432

Questions

1 a Who was Mr Cobbett (Source B line 2)?
  b What do you understand by 'a Dissenting or Methodist teacher' (Source C lines 13–14)?
2 How far does *The Times* comment in Source A suggest that class feeling might be a factor in the disturbances? Considering the likely knowledge and background of the writer, how useful is this as a source on the English countryside? What sources could be used to test the writer's claim that the English rural labourer had suffered a decline in living standards?

3 Compare the descriptions of the disturbances in Sources C and D and their reliability as evidence. How would you account for *The Times* correspondent having a more favourable attitude to the rebels than the Andover magistrates?

4 How does Source B compare with other sources in its suggestion of the reasons for the disturbances? How useful is it as an indication of why the revolt took place?

5 In your opinion, how accurate is Source E likely to be? How far does it support the impressions of the revolt given in Source A and Source C?

6 From these sources and any other evidence you know what do you think were the most important reasons for the 1830–31 revolt?[2]

Notes

1 *per se* – by itself
2 See, for example,
    Stevenson J 1979 *Popular Disturbances in England 1700–1870* Longman, Chap. 11
    Horn P 1987 *Life and Labour in Rural England, 1760–1850* Macmillan, Chap. 3
    An authoritative account of the revolt is given in
    Hobsbawm E J, Rudé G 1973 *Captain Swing* Penguin

3.2 Urban Experience: The Case For and Against Factory Reform

Child labour was not new in the Industrial Revolution, but the subjection of child and adult workers to factory discipline was. The most striking factories were the giant textile mills of the North, and the Factory Movement there agitated for legislation which would shorten children's hours and lead to a reduction of the adult working day. One of the most prominent campaigners, the MP Michael Sadler, introduced a bill to achieve the ten-hour day in 1832 and a House of Commons Select Committee was appointed under his chairmanship to investigate child labour in the mills. Following a General Election in 1832 when Sadler lost his seat, the government superseded this committee with a Royal Commission. This Commission carried out a more systematic enquiry but was generally considered to be less favourable to reform and aroused great resentment in the North. There was fierce debate between opposing interests and ideologies. How valid were the conflicting investigations and arguments?

A *Isaac Openshaw, a 23-year-old former mill worker answers questions posed by Sadler's Select Committee.*

Have you seen other boys crippled by standing and working those long days of labour? – Yes.

It is a common thing for them to get deformed in their limbs? – Yes.

Have you seen that occur in the mill in which you have been? – Yes.

You have been a considerable number of years in that mill, and observed that it has been the case? – Yes.

Have you found a number of children also to be ill by pursuing their labour to that degree? – Yes.

Were many of them obliged to leave the work who could not stand it? – Yes.

What is the longest time that you have ever worked in a mill? – Seventeen hours.

At what time did you begin then in the morning? – Four o'clock.

Parliamentary Papers 1831–32, Vol. XV, p 397

B *Part of Openshaw's examination for the Royal Commission of 1833.*

How many boys have you seen crippled by standing and working at piecing? – Three or four at Taylor's mill.

What are their names? – Robert France, Thomas Wallet, Josiah Taylor; I don't know the other lad's name.

How many other children do you know who have become crippled by working in mills; do you know several or many? – I dare say I have seen half a dozen . . .

What is the longest time you have ever worked? – From half past five in the morning till half past eight in the evening.

What intervals and rests did you have at those times? – Half an hour for breakfast, three quarters of an hour for dinner, and no time for bagging.

Did you ever work so long as seventeen hours in a mill, as you stated before the committee of the House of Commons? – I worked those hours as I say now.

Parliamentary Papers 1833, Vol. XX, pp 92–3

C *Comment from a radical local paper on two Royal Commissioners dining with Mr Marshall, a prominent Leeds mill-owner.*

It was not very regular, nor do we think very decent, for Judges, as the[y] styled themselves, to dine with one of the litigating parties . . . as Caesar's wife should be above suspicion, so should Lord Althorp's[1] Commissioners . . .

The Voice of the West-Riding, 15 June 1833

D *Mr John Hope MP argues against factory regulation on the second Reading of Sadler's Bill.*

. . . He did not propose to enter into any discussion as to the propriety or impropriety of interference with free labour. He believed it was admitted, on both sides of the House, that such interference generally was unwarrantable. He was willing to admit that the labour of children must, in some degree, be considered of a compulsory nature; but he considered that those very circumstances, which give such labour the character of compulsory, carried also with them a remedy for the evil of which the hon. Member complained, in the protection of their parents. He could not comprehend how it was possible, by legislative enactments, to supply the place of parental affections in behalf of the child . . . He doubted, in the first place, whether a case of necessity for parliamentary interference was fairly made out . . . It was material to look at the number of hours in which children were employed in other trades and manufactures. Children employed in the earthenware and porcelain manufactures worked from twelve to fifteen hours per day; file-cutters, nail-makers, forgers and colliers, worked for twelve hours per day; those employed in the manufacture of hosiery, and in lace manufactories, worked for twelve, thirteen, fourteen, and fifteen hours per day . . . He contended, therefore, that the children employed in cotton and other spinning factories were not subjected to greater labour than those employed in other manufactures, to whom no protection was to be afforded by this Bill . . .

It was obvious, that if they limited the hours of labour, they would, to nearly the same extent, reduce the profits of the capital on which the labour was employed. Under these circumstances, the manufacturers must either raise the price of the manufactured article, or diminish the wages of their workmen. If they increased the price of the article, the foreigner would enter into competition with them . . . He was informed that the foreign cotton manufacturers, and particularly the Americans, trod closely upon the heels of our manufacturers. If the latter were obliged to raise the price of their articles, the foreign markets would in a great measure be closed against them, and the increased price would also decrease the demand in the home market . . .

Hansard, 16 March 1832. Ser. 3, Vol. 11: 386–8, 392

E *Extracts from a condemnation of the factory system by John Fielden MP.*

The Parliament has passed an Act to abolish slavery in the English colonies, and not only the *name* but the essence of slavery; for, in that Act, it has taken care to provide that no negro shall work more hours in the week than *forty-five*, which is no more than seven and a half in the day. Now, then, if this Act of humanity was necessary, see how much more necessary is the eight-hour Act for the children of English *'free men.'* ...

... Did not the Commissioners, sent down into the north in 1833 by the Government, find that protection to the children was called for on grounds of bare humanity? ... In alluding to the cruelty of parents, who suffer their children to be overworked in factories for their own gain ... the Commissioners say that ...

'It appears in evidence that sometimes the sole consideration by which parents are influenced in making choice of a person under whom to place their children, is the amount of wages, not the mode of treatment, to be secured to them.' ...

Here, then, is the 'curse' of our factory-system: as improvements in machinery have gone on, the 'avarice of masters' has prompted many to exact more labour from their hands than they were fitted by nature to perform, and those who have wished for the hours of labour to be less for all ages than the legislature would even yet sanction, have had no alternative but to conform more or less to the prevailing practice, or abandon the trade altogether ...

Fielden J 1836 *The Curse of the Factory System,* pp 14, 18–20, 34–5

Questions

1 How far did Isaac Openshaw's evidence to the Royal Commission in Source B contradict the information he gave to the Select Committee in Source A or give a different impression?

2 What objections might be made to the Select Committee's method of questioning as seen in Source A?

3 Would the Royal Commissioners' acceptance of hospitality criticised in Source C invalidate their work to any extent?

4 **a** Compare the arguments in Sources D and E about how the manufacturing competition and the role of parents might make factory legislation necessary or harmful.

  b How valid was Hope's claim in Source D that children in 'cotton and other spinning factories were not subjected to greater labour than those employed in other manufactures' (lines 31–33)?[2]

5 Compare the types and method of argument in Sources D and E. Consider the values on which they are based and the kind of reasoning used. Which do you find more convincing and why?

Notes

1 Lord Althorp was a government minister
2 See, for example,
  Rule J 1986 *The Labouring Classes in Early Industrial England, 1750–1850* Longman, Chap. 5

3.3 The Impact of Legislation: The Anti-Poor Law Movement

Until 1834, poor relief was administered by individual towns and villages largely on the basis of laws made in the reign of Elizabeth I. Following complaints that the system was lax, over-generous and inefficient, the 1834 Poor Law Amendment Act established a more centralised scheme. Villages and small towns were grouped into unions, under Guardians of the Poor elected by local ratepayers, and recipients of poor relief (paupers) were to go into well-regulated workhouses. In practice, many continued to receive relief in their own homes, but new workhouses were built, hundreds of thousands of paupers entered them and a large-scale anti-Poor Law movement developed. Why did the new system generate such massive opposition?

A *Recommendations on how a pauper should be treated. This extract is taken from a Royal Commission report on the Poor Laws which provided the basis for government legislation.*

... his situation on the whole shall not be made really or apparently so eligible as the situation of the independent labourer of the lowest class. Throughout the evidence it is shown, that in proportion as the condition of any pauper class is elevated above the condition of independent labourers, the condition of the independent class is depressed; their industry is impaired, their employment becomes unsteady, and its remuneration in wages is diminished. Such persons, therefore, are under the strongest inducements to quit the less eligible class of labourers and enter the more eligible class of paupers.

Parliamentary Papers 1834, Vol. XXVII. In:
Bland A E, Brown P A, Tawney R H (eds) 1914
English Economic History: Select Documents
G Bell and Sons, p 662

B *From a petition against the new system of poor relief sent by the ratepayers of Chalfont St Giles, Buckinghamshire, May 1835.*

... we deem it an act of Great Injustice and cruelty for Old People to be dragged away from their Friends and relations and transported to some Distant dismal Workhouse to spend the remainder of their Wretched lives. And we likewise think it equally unjust and cruel for honest industrious labourers with their wife's and families if they cannot procure any work to be forced from their cottages, parting the man from his wife, and the parents from their children and sent to some distant Workhouse. In our humble opinions there is no line to be drawn (by forcing all into Workhouses) between the Industrious and the Idle. The following in our humble Opinions is a hard case. A Man with his wife and three children who bears a most industrious character and who worked for a Farmer threshing all

last winter, but who last Saturday fortnight discharged him in consequence of having no further employ for him till the Hay Season comes on, when he said he would employ him again. He Went Round the Parish the next week in search of work but could get none. On the Friday after he went to the Overseer who sent him to the Relieving Officer of the Amersham Union who told him that he should neither Relieve him nor find him Work but that they might all go to the Workhouse. If poor Industrious men who are an ornament to their Country are to be degraded and sent to the workhouse they will be obliged to give their homes up when they come out where must they go to, they will not have a place to put their heads in ...

PRO Ministry of Health Papers 12.380

C *From a report by the Guardians of the Maldon Union in Essex on the operation of the new Poor Law. This extract is taken from the Second Annual Report of the Poor Law Commissioners.*

The habits and behaviour of the labouring class are certainly improving. They feel they cannot now compel an overseer to relieve them as they used to do; they are consequently more cautious how they expend their earnings, and duly appreciate a good master; not captiously leaving their employ, as was too much the custom when they could demand relief from an overseer, without being subject to the searching enquiries they have now to submit themselves to ...

Parliamentary Papers 1836, Vol. XXIX, Part 1. In:
Brown A F J (ed) 1952 *English History from Essex Sources 1750–1900* Essex Record Office, pp 122–3

D *Report of a court case at Colchester, Essex.*

William Sallows was put to the bar, charged with assaulting Joseph Dennis, one of the serjeants at mace, on Wednesday evening last.

Mr Roy, the governor of the workhouse at St Mary at the walls [Colchester], stated that the prisoner with his wife and family were admitted into the house on Wednesday afternoon, and in a short time after their admission, the prisoner became very refractory, and refused to pay any regard to the rules and regulations of the house, and violently assaulted the son of witness. He, witness, felt it necessary to call in the aid of the police, and on Dennis endeavouring to restore order, prisoner violently assaulted him. Dennis corroborated the evidence of Mr Roy.

The prisoner in his defence said, he was not aware that he struck anyone; he only objected to being separated from his wife and family, and he should like to know who made that law.

Colchester and Chelmsford Gazette, 30 April 1836. In: Brown A F J (ed) 1952 *English History from Essex Sources 1750–1900* Essex Record Office, p 123

E *From a speech by a tailor at a Chartist meeting at Braintree, Essex.*

... In reference to the forcible separation of a man from his wife by the new poor-law, he said, that a measure more abominable never issued from a legislature ... I, exclaimed the speaker, have a wife, and I am not ashamed to say now, as I have said before, that I *love* her, and sooner than I will be torn from the bosom that has yielded consolation to me in all my trials and difficulties; sooner than I will be torn from that wife and from the children we love, I will *die* in the public streets. (Immense cheering.)

Essex, Herts & Kent Mercury, 20 November 1838

F *A workhouse, from 'Sketches in London' by J Grant.*

G *From the 'Weekly Dispatch', 18 March 1838.*

POVERTY AND CRIME – Anyone may, if he please, send a round of beef to Newgate, where it will be readily received, and promptly devoured; but if the person were to send a shilling's worth of bread and cheese to a Union workhouse it would be refused admittance, and his benevolence stigmatized as improper.

Wythen Baxter G R 1841 *The Book of the Bastiles,* John Stephens, p 127

H *This extract is taken from the radical Chartist newspaper, the 'Northern Star', 7 June 1845.*

The abolition of the *legal* relief for the un-employed; the denial of all relief, except on terms that would deter everyone but the soul-destroyed starving slave from accepting it; the institution of the 'workhouse *test*', with its workhouse dress – its *brand* of poverty – its classification – its separation of man and wife and mother and child – its 'scientific' dietaries, of skilly, bread, 4 ozs. of bacon for a whole week, and a morsel of cheese – its dysentery, hurrying off its inmates as if stricken with the plague; all this was well calculated to make the labourer *offer his services* for almost any amount of wage, sooner than subject himself to the cruelties that awaited him if he applied for aid in his necessity to those facetiously termed his *'guardians'*. And thus 'Philosophy' accomplished its aim. *It got at the wages of labour.* The Poor Law screw was well adapted to twine the labourer down to less and still less comfort. The less the 'share' of his pro-ductions kept for himself, the more there was for those who lived on his labour . . .

In: Hollis P (ed) 1973 *Class and Conflict in Nineteenth Century England 1815–1850* Routledge and Kegan Paul, p 212

Questions

1 What do you understand by
   a Newgate (Source G line 2)?
   b the 'workhouse *test*' (Source H line 5)?
   c the 'Philosophy' which accomplished its aims through the new Poor Law (Source H line 17)?
2 Why does Source A argue that the paupers' conditions should be less eli-gible (desirable) than those of other labourers?
3 In what ways do Source B and Sources D–H suggest that the Poor Law system was inhumane and unjust?
4 In what ways does Source C support the argument in Source H?
5 Evaluate each of Sources B–H as evidence on the operation of the new Poor Law. Consider the different ways in which the sources are useful and think about the probable motives of the writers and how far they are likely to be writing from first-hand knowledge.
6 How far do the sources suggest that the new Poor Law might be harmful as well as advantageous to the interests of the property-owning and employing classes?

3.4 Political Action: Why Did the Chartists Fail?

Many working class groups and causes – including anti-Poor Law demonstrators – were absorbed into the Chartist movement in the late 1830s. Although centred on the People's Charter with its call for manhood suffrage and other democratic demands, Chartists differed greatly over their ulti-mate aims and the means to attain them. Chartism concentrated on presenting huge petitions to Parliament in 1839, 1842 and 1848, and apparently gained greatest support when over three million people signed the 1842 demands. But the House of Commons dismissed all the petitions by large majorities and Chartists had to consider other means – strikes and forms of violent action. However, economic and military threats, like peaceful petitioning, brought no immediate gains. Why, with such seemingly massive support, did the Chartists apparently achieve so little?

A *An extract from the 1842 petition.*

Your Petitioners deeply deplore the existence of any kind of monopoly in this nation, and whilst they unequivocally condemn the levying of any tax upon the necessaries of life and upon those articles principally required by the labouring classes, they are also sensible, that the abolition of any one monopoly will never unshackle labour from its misery, until the people possess that power under which all monopoly and oppression must cease; and your petitioners respectfully mention the existing monopolies of the suffrage, of paper money, of machinery, of land, of the public press, of religion, of the means of travelling and transit, and a host of other evils too numerous to mention, all arising from class legislation.

Hansard, 3 May 1842. Ser. 3, Vol. 63

B *From a speech opposing the petition by the Whig MP and historian Macaulay.*

... I believe that universal suffrage would be fatal to all purposes for which government exists, and for which aristocracies and all other things exist, and that it is utterly incompatible with the very existence of civilisation. I conceive that civilisation rests on the security of property ... while property is insecure, it is not in the power of the finest soil, or of the moral or intellectual constitution of any country, to prevent the country sinking into barbarism, while, on the other hand, while property is secure, it is not possible to prevent

a country from advancing in prosperity ... ... What is the monopoly of machinery and land, which is to be remedied? ... if I understand this petition rightly, I believe it to contain a declaration, that the remedies for the evils of which it complains, and under which this country suffers, are to be found in a great and sweeping confiscation of property, and I am firmly convinced, that the effect of any such measure would be not merely to overturn those institutions which now exist, and to ruin those who are rich, but to make the poor poorer, and the amount of the misery of the country even greater, than it is now represented to be ...

Hansard, 3 May 1842. Ser. 3, Vol. 63: 46–8

C *The threat of Chartist violence assessed by General Napier who was in command of government troops in the North in 1839.*

24th July 1839
... The Chartists are numerous, and should one detachment be destroyed the soldiers would lose confidence; they would be shaken while the rebels would be exalted beyond measure. Their defeat finally would be certain, but much blood would be shed which need not be shed ...
6 August 1839
The plot thickens. Meetings increase and are so violent, and arms so abound, I know not what to think. The Duke of Portland tells me there is no doubt of any intended general rising. Poor people! They will suffer. They have set all England against them and their physical force:- fools! We have the physical force, not they. They talk of their hundred thousands of men. Who is to move them when I am dancing round them with cavalry, and pelting them with cannon-shot? What would their 100,000 men do with my 100 rockets wriggling their fiery tails among them, roaring, scorching, tearing, smashing all they came near? And when in desperation and despair they broke to fly, how would they bear five regiments of cavalry careering through

them? Poor men! Poor men! How little they know of physical force!

Napier W F P (ed) 1857 *The Life and Opinions of General Sir Charles James Napier*, Vol. II, pp 59, 69

D *Ben Brierley, a working class Lancashire writer whose father was a Chartist supporter, recalls Chartist activity during his childhood in Lancashire.*

In 1842 ... the 'great strike' took place, an event which some of our neighbours had been expecting a long time before, and were, in their way, prepared to meet. During the four years chartism had been rife, and the strike was its culmination. The *Northern Star*[1], the only newspaper that appeared to circulate anywhere, found its way weekly to the Cut Side[2], being subscribed for by my father and five others. Every Sunday morning these subscribers met at our house to hear what prospect there was of the expected 'smash-up' taking place. It was my task to read aloud so that all could hear at the same time; and ... comments ... were made ... A Republic was to take the place of the 'base, bloody, and brutal Whigs', and the usurpers of all civil rights, the Lords. The Queen was to be dethroned, and the president of a Republic take her place. This would be a very easy task. Ten thousand trained pikemen would sweep England through; and Hollinwood could furnish a contingent of at least a thousand ... Besides reading the *Northern Star* on Sunday mornings, my Saturday afternoons were occupied by more arduous work. I had to turn my father's grindstone whilst rebelliously-disposed amateur soldiers ground their pikes.

Brierley B 1886 *Home Memories and Recollections of Life* Abel Heywood, pp 24–5

Questions

1 What taxes were levied 'upon the necessaries of life and upon those articles principally required by the labouring classes' (Source A lines 4–6)?
2 What do you understand by 'the existing monopolies of the suffrage, of paper money, of machinery, of land, of the public press' (Source A lines 11–14)?
3 What problems do these sources suggest the Chartists faced in
   a petitioning Parliament?
   b using military force?
4 Using the evidence in this section and your own knowledge, try to work out whether these problems could have been overcome with the use of better tactics and organisation or whether the Chartists were bound to fail in mid-nineteenth-century Britain.[3]

Notes

1 *Northern Star* – Chartist newspaper which had a large circulation and formed a vital link between Chartist groups
2 Cut Side – houses where Brierley lived
3 See, for example,
   Royle E 1986 *Chartism* Longman, 2nd edn
   E Royle on *Chartism* in ReFRESH, 1986. Published from Alcuin College, University of York. Also printed in *New Directions in Economic and Social History* Macmillan, 1989
   Dinwiddy J R 1987 *Chartism* Historical Association

4 Conservative Government and Economic Reform 1815–46

4.1 Fiscal Reform Under Lord Liverpool: The Work of William Huskisson

Lord Liverpool's ministries which governed Britain from 1812 to 1827 inherited a complex system of customs duties. These duties had developed over several centuries and had been increased during the French Revolutionary and Napoleonic Wars (1793–1815), mainly to provide war finance and partly to protect home producers against foreign competition by raising the prices of imported goods. Such practice contradicted the theory of the most influential British economist of the Industrial Revolution – Adam Smith – who believed in minimal government regulation of the economy. Furthermore, increasing duties on imported goods seemed inappropriate as Britain could no longer feed herself and relied increasingly on imported food. Despite being responsible for the Corn Law of 1815, Liverpool's government subsequently moved towards *laissez faire* (government non-intervention), and this policy was continued and developed by William Huskisson as President of the Board of Trade from 1823. What were Huskisson's aims and why did he alter the British government's overseas trade policy?

A *Adam Smith explains the advantages of free trade.*

If a foreign country can supply us with a commodity cheaper than we ourselves can make it, better buy it of them with some part of the produce of our own industry employed in a way in which we have some advantage. The general industry of the country, being always in proportion to the capital which employs it, will not thereby be diminished; but only left to find out the way in which it can be employed with the greatest advantage. It is certainly not employed to the greatest advantage when it is thus directed towards an object which it can buy cheaper than it can make ...

According to the supposition, that a commodity could be purchased from foreign countries cheaper than it can be made at home, it could, therefore, have been purchased with a part only of the commodities, or, what is the same thing, with a part only of the price of the commodities, which the industry employed by an equal capital would have produced at home, had it been left to follow its natural course. The industry of the country, therefore, is thus turned away from a more to a less advantageous employment, and the exchangeable value of its annual produce, instead of being increased, according to the intention of the law-giver, must necessarily be diminished by every such regulation.

Smith A 1776 *The Wealth of Nations*. In: Tames R 1971 *Documents of the Industrial Revolution 1750–1850* Hutchinson, p 25

B *William Huskisson explains the government's policy over the removal of customs duties, 1825.*

It became us ... to watch the issue of each experiment, and not to attempt too much at once, until we had felt our way, and until the public were prepared to accompany us in our further progress ... Let any one go down to Brighton, and wander along the coast from thence to Hastings; I will undertake to say, that he shall most easily find, at every place he comes to, persons who will engage to deliver to him, within ten days or a fortnight, any prohibited article of manufacture, which he can name, and almost in any quantity, upon an advance of 30l. per cent, beyond the prime cost at Paris. What is the consequence of such a system? A number of families, that would otherwise be valuable and industrious members of society, exist, and train up their children, in a state of perpetual warfare with the law, till they insensibly acquire the habits and feelings of outlaws, standing rather in relation of pirates, than of fellow-subjects, to the rest of the community. And is this abominable system to be tolerated, not from any over-ruling necessity of upholding the revenue, nay, possibly, to the injury of the Exchequer, but merely because, in a few secondary branches of manufacture, we do not possess the same natural advantages, or the same degree of skill, as our neighbours? ...

The Speeches of the Right Honourable William Huskisson,
Vol. II, 1831, pp 328, 343

C *From 'Essays on Political Economy' written by Huskisson and published anonymously, 1830.*

The evils arising from a high price of food are exceedingly aggravated by the regulations which restrain the interchange of national productions for those of foreign countries. The British system has hitherto been that of favouring exportation, and discouraging importation as much as possible; a system founded in error, and one that is, in common times, quite impracticable ... The national prosperity is greatly prejudiced by the exclusive system, which desires to sell to other nations, and to limit the productions to be received in return. Exchanges cannot be carried on without receiving as well as giving a proper equivalent ... By receiving foreign productions in return for our own, then the whole quantity of necessaries, conveniences,

and luxuries is increased, labour is better rewarded, and the comforts of life are more easily obtained by all industrious classes in the community.

Essays on Political Economy 1830, pp 23–4

Questions

1 a Why, according to Adam Smith, was it in the national interest to buy foreign, rather than home-produced, goods if the foreign ones were cheaper?

b How in early nineteenth-century Britain was the 'general industry of the country' often 'directed towards an object which it can buy cheaper than it can make'?

c What did Smith consider to be the harmful consequences of this?

d What basic foodstuffs could Britain get more cheaply from abroad than from home production in the early nineteenth century?

2 What practical and theoretical arguments does Huskisson use to justify the extent and timing of the government's reductions in customs duties?

3 Compare Huskisson's arguments in favour of freer trade in Source C with Smith's in Source A.

4 From your own knowledge and the sources in this subsection, how far do you think Huskisson was concerned with making piecemeal reforms according to practical needs or attempting to achieve free trade according to fashionable economic theory?[1]

Notes

1 See text and topic books, for example,
Briggs A 1959 *The Age of Improvement* Longman, Chap. 4
Gash N 1979 *Aristocracy and People* Edward Arnold, Chap. 4

Hunt J W 1972 *Reaction and Reform 1815–1841* Collins, Chap. 4

Brown R, Daniels C 1980 *Nineteenth-Century Britain* Macmillan, contains extracts showing the change in historians' views on Toryism and economic policy in this period

For further interpretation of the policy of Liverpool's ministry, see

Gash N 1984 *Lord Liverpool* Weidenfeld and Nicolson

4.2 Peel and the Conservative Tradition – Continuity or Change?

The events of the French Revolution convinced many Englishmen of the need to preserve, or *conserve*, their way of government and avoid violent changes which might lead to chaos and bloodshed. The most important writer who stated this Conservative case against revolution – Edmund Burke – called himself a Whig but provided much of the basis for nineteenth-century Conservatism. The need to guard the English constitution against revolutionary dangers later helped to unify many conservative-minded men behind the government of Lord Liverpool and encouraged the idea of a Conservative party. An article in the *Quarterly Review* in 1830 declared its attachment to 'what is called the Tory, and which might with more propriety be called the Conservative Party'.

Two of the greatest leaders and orators within this group in the 1820s and 1830s were Canning and Peel, though both accepted a greater degree of reform than many Tory, or Conservative, supporters could approve. Peel has often been portrayed as the founder of the Conservative party, but he was suspected, as Disraeli put it, of attempting to create 'a party without principles'. How much continuity is there between Peel and earlier Tory and Conservative leaders and thinkers? Did Peel alter his party's principles?

A *Edmund Burke explains the strengths of the English constitution in his 'Reflections on the French Revolution'.*

Our constitution is a prescriptive constitution; it is a constitution whose sole authority is, that is has existed time out of mind ... And this is a choice not of one day, or one set of people, not a tumultuary and giddy choice; it is a deliberate election of ages and of generations; it is a constitution made by what is ten thousand times better than choice. It is made by the peculiar circumstances, occasions, tempers, dispositions, and moral, social and civil habitudes of the people, which disclose themselves only in a long space of time ...

... We are afraid to put men to live and trade each on his own private stock of reason; because we suspect that this stock in each man is small, and that the individuals would do better to avail themselves of the general bank and capital of nations, and of ages ...

Burke E 1790 'Reflections on the French Revolution'. In: White R J (ed) 1964 *The Conservative Tradition* Adam and Charles Black, pp 40–1

B *Canning opposes Parliamentary Reform in 1822.*

If the House [of Commons] has ... increased its power, is it, therefore, necessary that it should also become more popular in its formation? I should say – just the reverse. If it were to add to its real active governing influence, such an exclusively popular character and tone of action as would arise from the consciousness that it was the immediately deputed agent for the whole people, and the exclusive organ of their will – the House of Commons, instead of enjoying one-third of the power of the state, would, in a little time, absorb the whole. How could the House of Lords, a mere assembly of individuals, however privileged, and representing only themselves, presume to counteract the decisions of the delegates of the people? How could the Crown itself holding its power, as *I* should say, *for* the people, but deriving it altogether, as others would contend, *from* the people – presume to counteract, or hesitate implicitly to obey, the supreme authority of the nation assembled within these walls? ...

Hansard, 25 April 1822. Ser. 2, Vol. 7: 120. In: White R J (ed) 1964 *The Conservative Tradition* Adam and Charles Black, pp 138–9

C *The Duke of Wellington defends the existing House of Commons as Prime Minister in November 1830.*

He would ... say, that if at the present moment he had imposed upon him the duty of forming a Legislature for any country, and particularly for a country like this, in possession of great property of various descriptions, he did not mean to assert that he could form such a Legislature as they possessed now, for the nature of man was incapable of reaching such excellence at once; but his great endeavour would be, to form some description of legislature which would produce the same results ...

Hansard, 2 November 1830. Ser. 3, Vol. I: 53

D *Peel opposes the Whig government's third Reform Bill introduced in December 1831.*

... On this ground I take my stand, not opposed to a well-considered Reform of any of our institutions which need reform, but opposed to this Reform in our Constitution, because it tends to root up the feelings of respect, the feelings of habitual reverence and attachment, which are the only sure foundations of Government. I will oppose to the last the undue encroachments of that democratic spirit to which we are advised to yield without resistance ...

Hansard, 17 December 1831. Ser. 3, Vol. 9: 545. In: Gash N (ed) 1968 *The Age of Peel* Edward Arnold, pp 39–40

E *Peel explains his attitude to the Reform Act in the 'Tamworth Manifesto', 1834.*

... I consider the Reform Bill a final and irrevocable settlement of a great Constitutional question – a settlement which no friend to the peace and welfare of this country would attempt to disturb, either by direct or by insidious means.

Then, as to the spirit of the Reform Bill, and the willingness to adopt and enforce it as a rule of government: if, by adopting the spirit of the Reform Bill, it be meant that we are to live in a perpetual vortex of agitation ... I will not undertake to adopt it. But if the spirit of the Reform Bill implies merely a careful review of institutions, civil and ecclesiastical, undertaken in a friendly temper, combining, with the firm maintenance of established rights, the correction of proved abuses and the redress of real grievances, – in that case, I can for myself and colleagues undertake to act in such a spirit and with such intentions.

In: Gash N (ed) 1968 *The Age of Peel* Edward Arnold, pp 76–7

F *Peel addresses a Conservative audience at Merchant Tailors' Hall, 12 May 1838.*

... By conservative principles I mean, and I believe you mean, the maintenance of the Peerage and the Monarchy – the continuance of the just powers and attributes of King, Lords and Commons, in this country. By conservative principles I mean, a determination to resist every encroachment that can curtail the just rights and settled privileges of one or other of those three branches of the state. By conservative principles I mean, that co-existent with equality of civil rights and privileges, there shall be an established religion and imperishable faith, and that that established religion shall maintain the doctrines of the Protestant Church. By conservative principles I mean, a steady resistance to every project which would divert church property from strictly spiritual uses ... ... By conservative principles I mean, a maintenance of the settled institutions of church and state, and I mean also the maintenance, defence, and continuation of those laws, those institutions, that society, and those habits and manners which have contributed to mould and form the character of Englishmen ...

In: *The Peel Banquet, Speeches of the Rt Hon. Sir Robert Peel, Bart., Lord Stanley and Sir James Graham, Bart., at Merchant Tailors' Hall*, 1838, pp 9–10

G *Disraeli condemns Peel's politics in his novel 'Coningsby'.*

The Tamworth Manifesto ... was an attempt to construct a party without principles ... the awkward question naturally arose, what will you conserve? The prerogatives of the crown, provided they are not exercised; the independence of the House of Lords, provided it is not asserted; the ecclesiastical estate, provided it is regulated by a commission of laymen. Everything in short that is established, as long as it is a phrase and not a fact.

Disraeli B 1844 *Coningsby* Everyman's Library edn, J M Dent & Sons, 1911, pp 81–2

Questions

1 What do you understand by
   a 'a prescriptive constitution' (Source A line 1)?
   b 'feelings of habitual reverence and attachment' (Source D lines 6–7)?
   c 'those three branches of the state' (Source F line 9)?
   d 'the ecclesiastical estate' (Source G line 7)?
2 How do (a) Burke and (b) Canning justify the old English constitution including the unreformed House of Commons?
3 How far is Peel consistent or inconsistent in Sources D–F?
4 How different is his attitude from that of Wellington in Source C?

5 Compare Peel's attitude to reform and national institutions in Sources D–F with the arguments of Burke and Canning in Sources A and B, respectively. How far could any of the doctrines in Sources A and B be used to justify Peel's acceptance of constitutional change in the *Tamworth Manifesto*?
6 Why was the maintenance of 'the Protestant Church' and its property (Source F line 15) an important political issue when Peel spoke in 1838?
7 How accurate and how just are Disraeli's criticisms in Source G?

Notes

For this and later sections in this Chapter, see text and topic books, for example,
Briggs A 1959 *The Age of Improvement* Longman
Gash N 1979 *Aristocracy and People* Edward Arnold
Randell K H 1972 *Politics and the People 1835–1850* Collins
Blake R 1985 *The Conservative Party from Peel to Thatcher* Fontana
Coleman B 1988 *Conservatism and the Conservative Party in Nineteenth-Century Britain* Edward Arnold
Adelman P 1989 *Peel and the Conservative Party* Longman
The authoritative biography of Peel is:
Gash N 1986 *Sir Robert Peel*, 2nd edn, Longman

4.3 Were the Corn Laws Justifiable?

There had been restrictions on overseas trade in corn for centuries, but in the late seventeenth and early eighteenth centuries Britain was a corn *exporting* country. The eighteenth-century Corn Laws provided subsidies for exports as well as heavy taxes on imports when prices were low and allowed corn imports in freely or at nominal rates of duty if prices were high. With population growth and industrialisation in the late eighteenth century, however, Britain became a permanent grain importer. In these circumstances the 1815 Corn Law was controversial because it involved bans on corn imports: this kept British prices artificially high. The effect was modified in 1828 and 1842 by arrangements for import taxes to fall on a sliding scale as corn prices in Britain rose, but the 'Corn Laws' were still intended to keep up prices for the benefit of agriculturalists. Today we are familiar with Common Market policies which restrict imports and maintain artificially high food prices in order to subsidise farming interests and safeguard food supplies, but in early nineteenth-century Britain such a policy ran directly against the fashionable free-trade thinking (see section 4.1).

Richard Cobden, a mill-owner who became the MP for the cotton manufacturing town of Stockport, was the most prominent opponent of the laws and a leader of the Anti Corn Law League. Mr A S O'Brien was a little-known MP for the county seat of north Northamptonshire who made one of the most effective speeches in favour of the Corn Laws when their abolition was debated in 1846.

into the pockets of the landlord. Now do not suppose that I wish to deprive you of rents; I wish you to have your rents; but what I say is, don't come here to raise them by legislative enactments. I think you may have as good rents without a Corn-Law as with it; but what I say is this, that when you come here to raise the price of corn under the pretence of helping the farmer and the farm-labourer, whilst in reality you are only going to help yourselves, then, I say, you are neither dealing fairly by the farmer, nor yet by the country at large ...

I will now show you another view of the question. You have made the Corn-Law the subject of political outcry in the counties. You have made it a Church and State question, and at the same time you have made the farmers your stepping-stones to political power ...

There are 7,000,000 or 8,000,000 people without wheaten bread. If the people continue to descend in the scale of physical comfort, and to eat potatoes, the hope of moral improvement which the friends of humanity indulge must be altogether disappointed. The right hon. Gentleman the President of the Board of Trade said, that the importation of 600,000 quarters of wheat would be a national calamity; but how otherwise are the people to be supported? ...

In: Bright J, Thorold Rogers J E (eds) 1870 *Speeches on Questions of Public Policy*, Vol. I, Macmillan pp 45–62

A   Cobden attacks the Corn Law in Parliament, May 1843.

In supporting the present Corn-Law, you support a law which inflicts scarcity on the people. You do that, or you do nothing ... You cannot enhance the price of corn, or of any other article, but by restricting their supply. Are you justified in doing this, for the purpose of raising your price?

... If the Corn-Law operates to cause a profit at all, it also operates to put that profit

B   O'Brien defends the Corn Law, February 1846.

Supposing, then, that acting upon that axiom of buying in the cheapest and selling in the dearest market ... a wealthy man in England, furnished his house with paper-hangings from Paris. Supposing that he travelled in a continental carriage, that he purchased all his hardware from Germany; supposing all this, when he looked out of the window of his gaudy house, or his foreign-built carriage, what would he see? A vast multitude of unemployed starving Englishmen. And what would they say to him? 'We are poor English paper-stainers; we are Birmingham hardware-men; our trade has been taken away from us – what are we to do?' And what could be his reply? 'My good fellows, I have done the best I could to make you idle – to take all employment out of your hands – to leave you starving; but, believe me, I did it not from a bad motive.' What consolation would it afford them to be told, that all this happened; because on the 27th of January, 1846, Sir R. Peel propounded a doctrine in which all political economists were agreed, that labour might protect itself, and that we must buy in the cheapest market and sell in the dearest; and that the Legislature in abolishing protection was actuated by no consideration of self-interest, but solely with a desire that the great truths of political economy should have fair play? ... It is not a question now between cotton and corn, or corn against cotton. On that question we can tear each other to pieces, and the poor can understand us; but upon the great question of 'buying in the cheapest market, and selling in the dearest', how can we be consistent? ... I greatly doubt if this can be called a 'landlords question' ... It is not a question for the great landed proprietors – they who would be able to 'weather the storm' ... But the more I consider this question, the more am I satisfied it is a tenant-farmers' question ... Apply the precepts of your new philosophy to the tenant-farmer. Suppose prices fall in consequence - partly, perhaps, of an inundation of foreign corn - the tenant farmer says to his landlord, 'I hope, Sir, you will allow me a small abatement in my rent?' ... The landlord may reply, 'My good fellow, I am very sorry for you ... But we are told now by the Prime Minister that we are "to buy in the cheapest market, and sell in the dearest." There is a gentleman from the manufacturing districts with more capital than you, ready to invest in your farm. I really must look to my own family arrangements ...' Yes! unless the landlord acts towards his tenant a better part and with kindlier feeling than you are now prepared to act towards the whole agricultural body, the tenant-farmer must leave his farm ...

Hansard, 10 February 1846. Ser. 3, Vol. 83: 651–5

Questions

1 Why does Cobden argue that repeal of the Corn Laws will benefit poorer people and O'Brien that it will worsen their position?
2 How could landowners make the farmers their 'stepping-stones to political power' as Cobden alleged (Source A lines 27–8)?
3 How far do these sources suggest that the power and position of the land-owning class were the key issues in the debate over the repeal of the Corn Laws?
4 In many counties the major opposition to the Corn Laws came from tenant farmers. How can you explain this using the sources and any other available evidence?
5 How far do you think that the opinions of Cobden and O'Brien expressed in these sources can be explained by their constituencies, personal interests and background?

4.4 The Repeal of the Corn Laws – Did Peel Betray his Party?

Peel was responsible for the repeal of the Corn Laws in 1846. He acted then in response to the famine in Ireland where his government was taking relief measures which included the purchase of cheap foreign grain, but a majority of Conservative MPs voted against repeal and this led to the downfall of his ministry. Conservative opponents led by Lord George Bentinck and Disraeli bitterly accused him of betrayal: were they justified?

A *Peel discusses proposals to revise the existing Corn Laws in a speech in his Tamworth constituency at the 1841 General Election.*

... I come now, as I said, to the most important question of all – the introduction of foreign corn into this country. Gentlemen, I must here repeat the opinion which I have declared here before, and also in the House of Commons, that I cannot consent to substitute a fixed duty of 8s a quarter on foreign corn, for the present ascending and descending scale of duties ... And when I look at the burdens the land is subject to in this country, I do not consider the fixed duty of 8s a quarter on corn from Poland and Prussia and Russia, where no such burdens exist, a sufficient protection for it. Gentlemen, it is certainly a very tempting thing in theory to buy your corn at the cheapest market. But, gentlemen, before you adopt that theory in practice, you must, as a matter of common justice, compare the burthens on the land in other countries with the burthens on the land in this country. The land in this country is most heavily burthened ... Who pay the highway rates? Who pay the church rates? Who pay the poors' rate? Who pay the tithes? I say not, perhaps, altogether, but chiefly, the landed occupier of this country. And, gentlemen, if corn be the product of other land not subject to these burthens, it surely would not be just to the land of this country, which bears them all, to admit it at a low duty ... I deprecate a struggle on the subject of the Corn Laws, because I think, *as Lord Melbourne did last year*, the advantages are not sufficient to counterbalance the risk. And I ask your free suffrages with this frank and explicit declaration of my opinions.

Sir R Peel's Speech at the Nomination at Tamworth on Monday, 28 June 1841, pp 8, 18

B *Two agricultural experts, Professor Lindley and Dr Playfair, report to the government on the Irish famine, 15 November 1845.*

... we can come to no other conclusion than that one half of the actual potato crop of Ireland is either destroyed or remains in a state unfit for the food of man. We, moreover, feel it our duty to apprise you that we fear this to be a low estimate ...

It is also necessary to direct your attention to the quantity of seed potatoes which must be reserved for the coming year, if the cultivation of this plant is to be persevered in. We can state that, on an average, one-eighth of a crop is required for planting the same quantity of ground, so that in fact only three-eighths of the crop can in our view be at this moment assumed to be available as food.

In: *Memoirs by the Rt Hon Sir Robert Peel, Bart., M.P.*, Vol. II, John Murray, pp 171–2

C *Peel's Chancellor of the Exchequer, Goulburn, opposes his plans to repeal the Corn Laws. This extract is taken from a letter from Goulburn to Peel, 30 November 1845.*

I fairly own that I do not see how the repeal of the Corn Law is to afford relief to the distress with which we are threatened. I quite understand that if we had never had a Corn Law, it might be argued that we should now have had a larger supply in our own warehouses, or that from the encouragement given by a free trade in corn to the growth of it in foreign countries, we should have had a larger fund on which to draw for a supply. But I think it next to impossible to show that the abandonment of the law now could materially affect this year's supply, or give us any corn which will not equally reach us under the law as it stands ...

Peel's Memoirs, Vol. II, p 202. In: Gash N (ed) 1968 *The Age of Peel* Edward Arnold, p 129

D *Peel speaking in favour of Corn Law repeal in the House of Commons, 15 May 1846.*

... I do not rest my support of this Bill merely upon the temporary ground of scarcity in Ireland ... but I believe that scarcity left no alternative to us but to undertake the consideration of this question ... the real question at issue is the improvement of the social and moral condition of the masses of the population; we wish to elevate in the gradation of society that great class which gains its support by manual labour ...

Hansard, 15 May 1846. Ser. 3, Vol. 86: 695–6

E *Lord George Bentinck attacks Peel and his ministers for their repeal of the Corn Laws when speaking in debate on an Irish Coercion Bill.*

... I do think that the time has come when, by putting them in a minority, and by driving them from power, we ought to compel them to make atonement for the political treachery of which they have been guilty – for the dishonour which, by their conduct, they have brought upon Parliament – and for the dishonour which they have brought upon the country, as well as atonement for the treachery which they have shown towards the constituencies of the Empire.

Hansard, 8 June 1846. Ser. 3, Vol. 87: 184

F *Peel later justified his action in his 'Memoirs'.*

It appeared to me that all these considerations – the betrayal of party attachments – the maintenance of the honour of public men – the real interests of the cause of Constitutional Government, must all be determined by the answer which the heart and conscience of a responsible Minister might give to the question, What is that course which the public interests really demand? What is the course best calculated under present circumstances to diminish the risk of great suffering and the discontent which will be the consequence of that suffering if timely precautions which might be taken be neglected? ... I was not insensible to the evil of ... severing party connections, and of subjecting public men to suspicion and reproach and the loss of public confidence;

but I felt a strong conviction that such evils were light in comparison with those which must be incurred by the sacrifice of national interests to party attachments, and by deferring necessary precautions against scarcity of food for the purpose of consulting appearances and preserving the show of personal consistency ...

Peel's Memoirs, Vol. II, John Murray, pp 167–8

Questions

1 **a** Explain what is meant by a 'fixed duty' on foreign corn and an 'ascending and descending scale' (Source A lines 7–8).

   b Who was Lord Melbourne (Source A line 31)?

2 On what grounds did Peel justify the Corn Laws in Source A?

3 Why should Peel have thought Corn Law repeal would benefit 'that great class which gains its support by manual labour' (Source D lines 9–10)?

4 What reasons might Goulburn have for claiming that Corn Law repeal would not enable the Irish to get food in Source C?

5 In view of his statement in Source A, do you think Peel should have explained his change of opinion and called a General Election before repealing the Corn Laws or do you think the Irish situation justified his attempt to gain repeal as quickly as possible?

6 How far do you think Source F is an adequate answer to the charge of political treachery which Bentinck made in Source E?

5 Foreign Policy 1815–65

5.1 England's Role in Europe

As Foreign Secretary from 1812 to 1822, Castlereagh co-operated with other European governments to defeat France in the later stages of the Napoleonic Wars. In 1814 Britain, together with Russia, Prussia and Austria therefore made the Treaty of Chaumont as an alliance against Napoleon and this later formed the basis of the Congress System – a system of meetings between great European powers to discuss common interests and preserve peace. In later years, however, Castlereagh distanced himself from many of the attitudes and actions of the other European powers, and Canning (Foreign Secretary from 1822 to 1827) was keen to emphasise British independence and the breakdown of the Congress System. Palmerston, who subsequently managed British foreign policy as Foreign Secretary in 1830–34, 1835–41 and 1846–51 and as Prime Minister in 1855–58 and 1859–65, had been a strong follower of Canning and was also an enthusiastic exponent of British interests.

A *Castlereagh outlines his attitude to the Congress System in a State Paper of 1820.*

In this Alliance as in all other human Arrangements, nothing is more likely to impair or even to destroy its real utility, than any attempt to push its duties and obligations beyond the Sphere which its original Conception and understood Principles will warrant: – It was an union for the Reconquest and liberation of a great proportion of the Continent of Europe from the Military Dominion of France, and having subdued the Conqueror it took the State of Possession as established by the Peace under the Protection of the Alliance: – It never was however intended as an Union for the Government of the World, or for the Superintendence of the Internal Affairs of other States . . .

PRO Foreign Office Papers 7/148. In: Temperley H, Penson L M (eds) 1938 *Foundations of British Foreign Policy*, Cambridge University Press, p 54

B *Canning speaks about England's role in the world when receiving the Freedom of Plymouth, 1823.*

. . . I am contented to confess, that in the conduct of political affairs, the grand object of my contemplation is the interest of England.

Not, Gentlemen, that the interest of England is an interest which stands isolated and alone. The situation which she holds forbids an exclusive selfishness; her prosperity must contribute to the prosperity of other nations, and her stability to the safety of the world. But, intimately connected as we are with the system of Europe, it does not follow that we are therefore called upon to mix ourselves on every occasion, with a restless and meddling activity, in the concerns of the nations which surround us. It is upon a just balance of conflicting duties, and of rival, but sometimes incompatible, advantages, that a government must judge when to put forth its strength, and when to husband it for occasions yet to come ...

... Our present repose is no more a proof of inability to act, than the state of inertness and inactivity in which I have seen those mighty masses that float in the waters above your town, is a proof they are devoid of strength, and incapable of being fitted out for action. You well know, gentlemen, how soon one of those stupendous masses, now reposing on their shadows in perfect stillness, – how soon, upon any call of patriotism or of necessity, it would assume the likeness of an animated thing, instinct with life and motion – how soon it would ruffle, as it were, its swelling plumage – how quickly it would put forth all its beauty and its bravery, collect its scattered elements of strength, and awaken its dormant thunder ... such is England herself, while apparently passive and motionless she silently concentrates the power to be put forth on an adequate occasion. But God forbid that that occasion should arise.

In: Therry R (ed) 1828 *The Speeches of the Rt Hon George Canning*, Vol. VI, James Ridgway, pp 421–4

C *Palmerston explains his foreign policy in 1848.*

... I hold that the real policy of England – apart from questions which involve her own particular interests, political or commercial – is to be the champion of justice and right; pursuing that course with moderation and prudence ... in pursuing that course ... she will never find herself altogether alone ...

We have no eternal allies, and we have no perpetual enemies. Our interests are eternal and perpetual, and those interests it is our duty to follow. ... And if I might be allowed to express in one sentence the principle which I think ought to guide an English Minister, I would adopt the expression of Canning, and say that with every British Minister the interests of England ought to be the shibboleth of his policy.

Hansard, 1 March 1848. Ser. 3, Vol. 97: 122–3

Questions

1 **a** What do you understand by 'the Peace' (Source A line 11)?
  b Who wished to make the union one 'for the Government of the World' (Source A line 14)?
2 Compare the views on England's foreign commitments and international relations expressed by the foreign secretaries in these sources.
3 How far do the beliefs Palmerston expresses in Source C explain his frequent unpopularity among foreign governments and popularity at home?
4 How far did the statesmen who managed British foreign policy later in the nineteenth century follow the principles and policies Canning outlined in Source B?

Notes

For this and later sections of this chapter, see, Ward D R 1972 *Foreign Affairs 1815–1865* Collins
Chamberlain M E 1980 *British Foreign Policy in the Age of Palmerston* Longman
Chamberlain M E 1988 *'Pax Britannica'? British Foreign Policy 1789–1914* Longman

5.2 Palmerston's Diplomacy: Mehemet Ali and France

Mehemet Ali, the Albanian adventurer who ruled Egypt, took over large areas of the Middle East, including Palestine and Syria, in 1831–32. Continuing his advance towards the Turkish capital, Constantinople, he threatened the Turkish Empire and therefore the whole balance of power around the Mediterranean. Despite Palmerston's wish to intervene, the British government had been unable to take action, and Russia made the most of her opportunity to assist the Turkish Sultan and gain diplomatic influence at Constantinople.

Her reward – the famous Treaty of Unkiar Skelessi in 1833 – gave the Russian government considerable wartime control over the vital straits of water between the Black Sea and the Mediterranean. With a renewed crisis in 1839 Palmerston soon took the diplomatic initiative, intervening together with other powers to oppose Mehemet Ali and assist the Turkish government so as to counterbalance the Russian influence. This policy raised the danger of war with France who supported Mehemet Ali, but the outcome is generally considered to be one of Palmerston's greatest triumphs. How substantial was his success and how was it achieved?

A *Palmerston outlines British policy in a letter to Lord Beauvale, the British Ambassador at Vienna, 28 June 1839.*

... It appears then to Her Majesty's Government, that there can be no end to the danger with which these affairs menace the peace of Europe, until Mehemet Ali shall have restored Syria to the direct authority of the Sultan; shall have retired into Egypt; and shall have interposed the Desert between his troops and authorities and the troops and authorities of the Sultan. But Mehemet Ali could not be expected to consent to this, unless some equivalent advantage were granted to him; and this equivalent advantage might be hereditary succession in his family to the Pashalic of Egypt ...

Correspondence relative to the Affairs of the Levant, I, p 119. *Parliamentary Papers 1841*, Vol. XXIX

B *From the Convention for the Pacification of the Levant, 15 July 1840.*

His Highness the Sultan having come to an agreement with their Majesties the Queen of the United Kingdom of Great Britain and Ireland, the Emperor of Austria ... the King of Prussia, and the Emperor of all the Russias, as to the conditions of the arrangement which it is the intention of His Highness to grant to Mehemet Ali ... If the Pasha of Egypt should refuse to accept the ... arrangement ... Their Majesties engage to take, at the request of the Sultan, measures concerted and settled between Them, in order to carry that arrangement into effect ...

[The Sultan] promises to grant to Mehemet Ali, for himself and for his descendants in the direct line, the administration of the Pashalic of Egypt; and His Highness promises, moreover, to grant to Mehemet Ali, for his life, with the title of Pasha of Acre ... the administration of the southern part of Syria ... [on] condition, that Mehemet Ali ... withdraw immediately from Arabia ... and from all other parts of the Ottoman Empire which are not comprised within the limits of Egypt, and within those of the Pashalic of Acre, as above defined.

Correspondence relative to the Affairs of the Levant, I, pp 691, 692, 696. *Parliamentary Papers 1841*, Vol. XXIX. In: Anderson M S 1970 *The Great Powers and the Near East 1774–1923* Edward Arnold, pp 49–51

C *From the report of a conversation with the French Prime Minister, Thiers, by Henry Bulwer, the British* chargé d'affaires *in Paris, 27 July 1840.*

[Thiers] said ... that the Government of France must satisfy the people that in its isolated position it was still strong enough to protect the honour and interests of the country; that, consequently, measures of that kind (meaning armaments, I presume), would be necessary. That they were inevitable, and never without danger ...

Correspondence relative to the Affairs of the Levant, II, p 40. *Parliamentary Papers 1841*, Vol. XXIX

D *From a dispatch from Palmerston to Bulwer, 22 September 1840.*

Notwithstanding the mysterious threatening with which Thiers has favoured us, I still hold to my belief that the French Government will be too wise and prudent to make war; and various things which come to me from different quarters confirm me in that belief ... But if Thiers should again hold to you the language of menace, however indistinctly and vaguely shadowed out, pray retort upon him to the full extent of what he may say to you, and with that skill of language which I know you to be the master of, convey to him in the most friendly and unoffensive manner possible, that if France throws down the gauntlet we shall not refuse to pick it up; and that if she begins a war, she will to a certainty lose her ships, colonies, and commerce before she sees the end of it; that her army of Algiers will cease to give her anxiety, and that Mehemet Ali will just be chucked into the Nile. I wish you had hinted at these topics when Thiers spoke to you; I invariably do so when either Guizot or Bourqueney begin to swagger ...

In: The Rt Hon Sir H L Bulwer 1870 *The Life of Henry John Temple, Viscount Palmerston*, Vol. II, Richard Bentley, pp 327–8

E *Extract from the Straits Convention, July 1841.*

Their Majesties the Emperor of Austria ... the King of the French, the Queen of the United Kingdom of Great Britain and Ireland, the King of Prussia, and the Emperor of all the Russias ... have resolved to comply with the invitation of His Highness the Sultan, in order to record in common, by a formal Act, their unanimous determination to conform to the ancient rule of the Ottoman Empire, according to which the passage of the Straits of the Dardanelles and of the Bosphorus is always to be closed to foreign ships of war, so long as the Porte is at peace ...

Correspondence relative to the Affairs of the Levant, III, p 324. *Parliamentary Papers 1841*, (Session 2) Vol. VIII. In: Anderson M S 1970 *The Great Powers and the Near East 1774–1923* Edward Arnold, pp 51–2

Questions

1 Compare Palmerston's policy as stated in Source A with the terms of the international convention in Source B. How near was it to the final outcome in 1840–41?
2 Compare the threats expressed by Thiers and Palmerston in Sources C and D.
3 Palmerston has often been described as following a policy of diplomatic brinkmanship. Using the evidence in this section and your own knowledge assess how far this was true in the Middle East crisis of 1839–41. How great was the danger of Palmerston's policy involving Britain in war?[1]
4 What advantages did Britain gain from the Straits Convention?

Notes

1 A useful narrative and analysis is given in: Ridley J 1972 *Palmerston* Panther, Chaps. 16, 17

5.3 Palmerston and the Rights of the British Citizen Abroad

Palmerston is well known for his defence of British citizens and commercial interests abroad. The most famous, or notorious, case was his support for British subjects in dispute with the Greek government – Don Pacifico, a Jewish money-lender who claimed compensation after an Athenian mob burnt his house; Finlay, a Scottish historian whose garden had been taken without compensation for the Greek royal palace; and a blacksmith from the British-owned Ionian Islands who was arrested and allegedly tortured by Greek police. These grievances were all some years old in late 1849 when Palmerston ordered a British fleet returning from Turkey to take action at Athens. Was he justified?

A *Letter to Palmerston from Sir Edmund Lyons, the British Ambassador to Greece about the attack on Don Pacifico's house at Easter 1847.*

... there is a great distinction between a common burglary and a protracted attack upon a large and conspicuous house in the middle of the day by several hundred persons, who were aided, instead of being repressed, by soldiers and gendarmes, and who were accompanied and encouraged, if not headed, by persons whose presence naturally induced a belief amongst the soldiers and the mob, that the outrages they were committing would be indulgently treated by the Government.

Correspondence respecting the demands made upon the Greek Government, I, p 53. *Parliamentary Papers 1850*, Vol. LVI

B *Palmerston's instructions to Wyse, the next Ambassador to Greece, 3 December 1849.*

I have desired the Admiralty to instruct Sir William Parker to take Athens on his way back from the Dardanelles, and to support you in bringing at last to a satisfactory ending the settlement of our various claims upon the Greek Government. You will of course, in conjunction with him, persevere in the *suaviter in modo* as long as is consistent with our dignity and honour, and I measure that time by days – perhaps by some very small number of hours. If, however, the Greek Government does not strike, Parker must do so ... He should, of course, begin by reprisals; that is, by taking possession of some Greek property; but the King would probably not much care for our taking hold of any merchant property, and the best thing, therefore, would be to seize hold of his little fleet, if that can be done

handily. The next thing would be a blockade of any or all of his ports; and if that does not do, then you and Parker must take such other steps as may be requisite, whatever those steps may be.

In: The Hon Evelyn Ashley M. P. 1876, *The Life of Henry John Temple, Viscount Palmerston*, Vol. I, Richard Bentley, pp 183–4

C *The Conservative leader, Lord Stanley, attacks Palmerston's policy in the House of Lords.*

... the course which the Government has pursued by its violence ... has endangered, the continuance of our friendly relations with other Powers ... I ask your Lordships to state whether, amongst the claims urged against the weak and feeble state of Greece ... there are not some which are either doubtful in point of justice, or exaggerated in point of amount ... of all the various cases which have been pressed upon the Greek Government on the late occasion, there is but one – that of Mr Finlay – in which the claimant has any right to be considered as a person of character and respectability ...

... The demand made by Mr Finlay ... was ... about 1,500l. for a piece of ground which cost him 10l. or 20l. ...

... when we come to look at M. Pacifico's bill of costs, it is really one which passes credibility ... listen to the amount of a single couch in his drawing room: – 1 large couch in solid mahogany ... 2 pillows and cushion also ... in silk and wool covering, embroidered in real gold ...

Total for one couch 170l. Now, I doubt if many of your Lordships have in your houses (I am sure I have not in mine) furniture of this gorgeous description ...

Hansard, 17 June 1850. Ser. 3, Vol. III: 1294–316

D *Palmerston defends his position in the House of Commons.*

... The country is told that British subjects in foreign lands are entitled – for that is the meaning of the resolution – to nothing but the protection of the laws and tribunals of the land in which they happen to reside ...

Now, I deny that proposition; and I say it is a doctrine on which no British Minister ever yet has acted, and on which the people of England never will suffer any British minister to act ...

I say then, that if our subjects abroad have complaints against individuals, or against the Government of a foreign country, if the courts of law of that country can afford them redress, then, no doubt, to those courts of justice the British subject ought in the first instance to apply; and it is only on a denial of justice, or upon decisions manifestly unjust, that the British Government should be called upon to interfere. But there may be cases in which no confidence can be placed in the tribunals, those tribunals being, from their composition and nature, not of a character to inspire any hope of obtaining justice from them ...

... But, it is said, M. Pacifico should have applied to a court of law for redress. What was he to do? Was he to prosecute a mob of five hundred persons? ... Where was he to find his witnesses? Why, he and his family were hiding or flying, during the pillage, to avoid the personal outrages with which they were threatened ...

Whether M. Pacifico's statement of his claim was exaggerated or not, the demand [from the British Government to the Greek Government] was not for any particular amount of money. The demand was, that the claim should be settled ...

... was there anything so uncourteous in sending, to back our demands, a force which should make it manifest to all the world that resistance was out of the question? Why it seems to me, on the contrary, that it was more consistent with the honour and dignity of the Government on whom we made those demands, that there should be placed before their eyes a force, which it would be vain to resist, and before which it would be no indignity to yield. If we had sent merely a frigate and a sloop of war, or any force with which it was possible their forces might have matched, we should have placed them in a more undignified position by asking them to yield to so small a demonstration ...

I therefore fearlessly challenge the verdict which this House, as representing a political, a commercial, a constitutional country, is to give on the question now brought before it ...

Whether, as the Roman, in days of old, held himself free from indignity, when he could say *Civis Romanus sum*; so also a British subject, in whatever land he may be, shall feel confident that the watchful eye and the strong arm of England, will protect him against injustice and wrong.

Hansard, 25 June 1850. Ser. 3, Vol. 112: 381–444

Questions

1 With which 'other Powers' would Palmerston's action endanger 'the continuance of ... friendly relations' (Source C line 3)?
2 On what general grounds does Palmerston support the right of a British government to intervene on behalf of British citizens abroad?
3 Compare the arguments of Stanley and Palmerston about the use of extensive armed force over the case of Don Pacifico.
4 There was no telegraph between London and Greece: information and instructions were sent by letter between the Foreign Office and the British Embassy in Athens. Using Sources A and B and any other evidence known to you try to work out how far British actions in Greece were decided by Palmerston on the one hand or resident British diplomats abroad on the other.
5 How far do you think Palmerston's policy was right or wrong?[1]

Notes

1 For a detailed account, see:
   Ridley J 1972 *Palmerston* Panther, Chaps. 26, 27

5.4 Was it Necessary to Fight Russia in the Crimean War?

Britain fought Russia in the Crimean War of 1854–56 primarily to safeguard the Turkish Empire against Russian threats. However, many politicians such as Lord John Russell saw a wider Russian menace. How reasonable were their fears?

A *Russell explains the danger from Russia.*

Russia has, since the commencement of the century, increased her power more than any other Power of Europe. She has upwards of 60,000,000 of inhabitants, and has an army of 800,000 men – I speak of a time of peace, and before the outbreak of the war ... In Poland she has erected six or seven fortresses, of at least equal strength with Sebastopol ... In the Baltic we find from the discoveries made last year ... that a great plan of fortification had been undertaken ... In Germany she has connected herself with many of the smaller Princes by marriage ...

Hansard, 24 May 1855. Ser. 3, Vol. 138: 1082–3

B *Russell is asked about the government's object in fighting the Crimean War.*

My answer to that question must be a very general one, that it is still as it has been – as security for Turkey against Russia, and, therefore, a security for the peace of Europe. I cannot believe that if Russia were left to work her way undisturbedly to the capital of the Turkish Empire – making, perhaps, a little progress in 1855, great progress ten years hence, and still further twenty years hence – the independence of Europe would be secure. Every one has read the incident – and I believe it has lately appeared in the public papers – of

the first Napoleon, when engaged with the Emperor Alexander in considering this great question, calling for a map, putting his finger on Constantinople, and, after some moments' meditation, exclaiming, 'Constantinople! No, it is the empire of the world.' I remember, too, another great man, the Duke of Wellington, saying – I cannot remember exactly on what occasion – that if, in addition to the forces of Russia in the Baltic, she were also by means of Constantinople to obtain the command of the Mediterranean, she would be too strong for the rest of the world. That, I believe, is not only the recognised opinion of great statesmen, but it is also the pervading sense of this country, and we must not, therefore, allow Russia, either by a simulated peace or by open war to effect the conquest of Constantinople.

Hansard, 5 June 1855. Ser. 3, Vol. 138: 1476–7

C *Richard Cobden questions the need for war in 1856.*

But we talk of this as a war which affects the interest of all Europe; and we hear the phrases 'Balance of Power' and 'International Law' frequently repeated, as though we were enforcing the edicts of some constituted authority. For a century and a half we have been fighting, with occasional intermissions, for the Balance of Power, but I do not remember that it has ever been made the subject of peaceful diplomacy, with a view to the organisation of the whole of Europe. Now, if such a pact or federation of the States of Europe as is implied by the phrases 'Balance of Power' or 'International Law' should ever be framed, it must be the work of peace, and not of war. In the present case, our government has entered into war on the assumption that the European Balance has been, and still is, endangered by the ambition of Russia. Has the rest of Europe ever been, as a whole, consulted in a time of peace, and in a deliberate manner, upon this danger, and invited to take a part in averting

it? If not, what shall we say of our government, or our governing class, or diplomacy in
general? Now, assuming again that I occupied
the position of our government, and were in
earnest in my fears for Europe and attached a
real meaning to those phrases just quoted, I
should appeal not only to Germany, but to all
the States, small as well as great, of the Continent, for such a union would prevent the
possibility of any act of hostility from the
common enemy. This is the work of peace;
and to this end, with the views and responsibilities of the government, I should
address myself. If I found that I failed to
impart my apprehensions to the other nations
in Europe, – if they declined to form part of
a league, or confederation against Russian
encroachments, I should be disposed to
reconsider my own views on the subject, and
to doubt whether I might not have been led
away by an exaggerated alarm. In that case, at
least, I would forego the quixotic mission of
fighting for the liberties of Europe, and pursue
a policy more just towards the interests, and
more consistent with the prosperity, of the
people whose welfare I was more especially
charged to promote.

Cobden R 1856 'What next – and next?' In: *Political
Writings of Richard Cobden*, Vol. II, James Ridgway,
pp 205–6

Questions

1 What was the significance of Sebastopol
   (Source A line 8)?
2 What do you understand by the 'Balance
   of Power' (Source C line 3)?
3 Why does Russell argue that Britain
   needed to fight Russia and how far does
   Cobden counter his arguments?
4 How far does Cobden envisage the type
   of international peace-keeping organisations which have been used in the
   twentieth century in Source C? How far is
   he putting forward a practical programme for action or just showing the
   weakness of the government's justifica-
   tion for the war?
5 Russell was in the Cabinet which took
   Britain into the Crimean War, and
   Sources A and B are taken from speeches
   he made as a member of the government
   fighting the war in 1855. Cobden was a
   radical who wanted free trade and who
   believed this might lead to greater international prosperity and more peaceful
   relations between states. How far do you
   think these circumstances or view-points
   account for the opinions they express?

6 Gladstone and his First Ministry

The politics of 1868–80 were characterised by a struggle between Gladstone and Disraeli. When the two men led their party followers in battle over parliamentary reform in the House of Commons in 1866–67 Disraeli achieved a tactical triumph, but it was the Liberal side under Gladstone which won the ensuing general election in 1868. Gladstone then went on to head one of the nineteenth century's great reforming ministries from 1868 to 1874. His rivalry with Disraeli was often a contest between contrasting styles and conflicting ambitions rather than one about political substance, but their differences over foreign policy and morality were deep and bitter.

6.1 Gladstone and Disraeli – Two Views of Foreign Policy

A *From an article written by Gladstone while Prime Minister and published anonymously in 'The Edinburgh Review', October 1870.*

The world-wide cares and responsibilities with which the British people have charged themselves are really beyond the ordinary measure of human strength; and, until a recent period, it seemed the opinion of our rulers that we could not do better than extend them yet further, wherever an opening could easily or even decently be found . . .

We have ceased, or are fast ceasing, from the feverish contest for influence all over the world; and we are learning that that influence which is least courted, and least canvassed for, comes the quickest, and lives the longest. If we no longer dream of foreign acquisitions, we are content in having treaties of mutual benefit with every nation upon earth; treaties not written on parchment, but based on the permanent wants and interests of man, kept alive and confirmed by the constant play of the motives which govern his daily life, and thus inscribing themselves, in gradually deepening characters, on the fleshly tablets of the heart . . .

One accomplishment yet remains needful to enable us to hold without envy our free and eminent position. It is that we should do as we would be done by; that we should seek to found a moral empire upon the confidence of the nations, not upon their fears, their passions, or their antipathies. Certain it is that a new law of nations is gradually taking hold of the mind, and coming to sway the practice, of the world; a law which recognises independence, which frowns upon aggression, which favours the pacific, not the bloody settlement of disputes, which aims at permanent and not temporary adjustments; above all, which recognises as a tribunal of paramount authority, the general judgment of civilised mankind . . .

'Germany, France and England.' *The Edinburgh Review*, October 1870, pp 591–3

B *From Disraeli's speech to the National Union of Conservative Associations at the Crystal Palace, 1872.*

If you look to the history of this country since the advent of Liberalism, 40 years ago, you will find that there has been no effort so continuous, so subtle, supported by so much energy, and carried on with so much ability and acumen, as the attempts of Liberalism to effect the disintegration of the Empire . . .

When you return to your homes, to your counties and your cities, you must tell to all those whom you can influence that the time is at hand, that, at least, it cannot be far distant (loud and continued cheers) when England will have to decide between national and cosmopolitan principles. The issue is not a mean one. It is whether you will be content to be a comfortable England, modelled and moulded upon Continental principles and meeting in due course an inevitable fate, or whether you will be a great country – an imperial country – a country where your sons, when they rise, will rise to paramount positions, and obtain not merely the respect of their countrymen, but command the respect of the world. (Loud cheers.)

The Times, 25 June 1872

Questions

1 What do you understand by
   a 'treaties not written on parchment' (Source A lines 16–17)?
   b 'a new law of nations' (Source A line 31)?
   c 'cosmopolitan principles' (Source B lines 13–14)?
2 What were the main territories of the British Empire by 1872? In what ways could it be argued that Liberalism had attempted to 'effect the disintegration' of this Empire in the forty years before 1872 (Source B line 7) and how far do you think the accusation was justified?[1]
3 Compare the feelings and values to which Gladstone and Disraeli are appealing.
4 Source A was published anonymously while Source B was delivered to a large party meeting. Evaluate the statements as expressions of the two politicians' views and explain their differing use to the historian.

Notes

1 First consult an historical atlas, for example, *The Penguin Atlas of World History* Vol. 2, Penguin, 1978
Not all textbooks include much coverage of the Empire, but there are useful sections in:
Read D 1979 *England 1868–1914* Longman, Chap. 9
Wood A 1982 *Nineteenth Century Britain 1815–1914* Longman, 2nd edn, Chap. 24
A fuller account is given in:
Eldridge C C 1978 *Victorian Imperialism* Hodder and Stoughton

6.2 The 1870 Education Act – The Influence of Pressure Groups on Legislation

There was widespread agreement that elementary education must be expanded in Gladstone's first ministry but there was no consensus about how it should be done. Existing elementary schools were largely provided by religious societies which raised money by voluntary contributions and were then subsidised by government grants. Not surprisingly, the Anglicans raised the most money, received the largest grants and were able to maintain the most schools. These were then geared to teaching Church of England doctrines as well as the basics of reading, writing and arithmetic.

The National Education League, founded in early 1869 and supported by many Nonconformists, campaigned for a very different type of schooling. In turn, the League was opposed by the National Education Union and many Conservative leaders who were more favourable to the Anglican-dominated 'voluntary' system. Forster, the government minister responsible for education, who introduced the 1870 Education Act was driven to complain that 'the religious difficulty' had 'kept the country in comparative ignorance for ten years past' and that parliamentarians were not thinking of 'the poor little children'.

A   *From a lecture by Francis Adams, the Secretary of the National Education League.*

We charge, therefore, against the present system of state-aided schools, that it is utterly insufficient in quantity; that the quality and amount of instruction given is wholly disproportionate to the labour and cost, and inadequate to the need of the scholars; that it is accidental, uncertain, and dependent upon partial and isolated effort; that it imposes upon a few the duty which should be recognized by all ...

The present system of aid from Parliamentary grants was intended to be an experiment ... The National Education League proposes to supplement this system by one which shall be national, universal, and certain – which shall be independent of the accidents of wealth and benevolence – which shall impose upon all an obligation which should be felt by all ... We hope to attain these results by making education national, compulsory, unsectarian and free. *Imprimis*, we hope to found a national system ... What do we mean by a national system? We mean one which shall be supported by the nation, and shall belong to the nation. But it is said we are a country of different sects and different beliefs – you cannot found any 'national' system which does not take account of these. That is a very good argument against the existence of a National Church; but it is no argument against a system of national education, which has nothing to do with creeds and tenets ...

'Lecture on Education', delivered at Huntingdon, 17 February 1870, pp 8–9

B   *Lord Robert Montagu, the Conservative spokesman, speaking on the Education Bill in the House of Commons.*

There was at present great voluntary support to schools; it was a matter of charity; and the burden was very unequal, because it varied according to the charitable feeling of individuals. Even these persons, at times, were conscious of the burden and of its inequality; so that under this Bill many would resort to rates to save their subscriptions ... such a system would put an end not only to voluntary subscriptions but also, as a consequence, to that interest in education which ought to be felt throughout the whole community ...

Hansard, 17 February 1870. Ser. 3, Vol. 199: 473

The late Report on the state of education in four of our great towns had showed that the Church had done nearly everything there. It had established good schools, and carried them on quietly and unostentatiously for years. If anyone desired to know which religious body was the most earnest in the cause of education, let him consult any one of the Reports of the Committee of Council, and he would see how Churchmen had laboured, what large sums they had expended, and how many schools they maintained ...

Hansard, 15 March 1870. Ser. 3, Vol. 199: 1981

C   *Forster speaking on the introduction and second reading of his Bill.*

We have said that we must have provision for public elementary schools. The first question then is, by whom is it to be made? ... To see, then, whether voluntary help will be forthcoming we give a year[1] ... If that zeal, if that willingness, does not come forward to supply the schools that are required, then the children must no longer remain untaught, and the State must step in ... I have said that there will be compulsory provision where it is wanted ... but not otherwise ... How do we propose to apply it? By school Boards elected by the district. We have already got the district; we have found out the educational want existing in it – we see that the district must be supplied – we have waited in the hope that some persons would supply it; they have not done so. We, therefore, say that it must be supplied; but by whom? ... Voluntary local agency has failed, therefore our hope is to invoke the help of municipal organization. Therefore, where we have proved the educational need we supply it by local administration – that is, by means of rates aided by money voted by Parliament, expended under local management, with central inspection and control. I wish to be frank with the House, and I therefore say that undoubtedly this proposal will affect a large portion of the kingdom. I believe it will affect almost all the towns, and a great part of the country.

Hansard, 17 February 1870. Ser. 3, Vol. 199: 450–1

We were also determined that, while not discouraging religion, we would not treat one religious sect with greater indulgence than another . . . It is quite true that there are throughout the country a vast number of Church schools; but it is not our fault that they are in existence; and it is allowed by all who take an interest in the subject that we must not destroy before we build up. If, by passing this measure, we destroy the present educational agencies, it will be long before we could do as much good as we should have done harm; and, therefore, as a friend of education, and of education only, I was anxious that we should help every person, whether he belonged to the Church of England or not, who was willing to spend either his time or his money in promoting education among his poorer neighbours . . .

Hansard, 14 March 1870. Ser. 3, Vol. 199: 1948

D   *A cartoon from 'Punch', 2 July 1870.*

"OBSTRUCTIVES."

Mr. Punch (*to* Bull A 1). "YES, IT'S ALL VERY WELL TO SAY, 'GO TO SCHOOL!' HOW ARE THEY TO GO TO SCHOOL WITH THOSE PEOPLE QUARRELLING IN THE DOORWAY? WHY DON'T YOU MAKE 'EM 'MOVE ON'?"

Questions

1 **a** What do you understand by 'unsectarian' education (Source A line 21)?
  b Who are the obstructive people quarrelling in the doorway in Source D?
2 What were the merits of the voluntary system according to Montagu (Source B) and the disadvantages according to Adams (Source A)? How valid do you think their views were?
3 To what extent does a comparison of the statements from Forster, Adams and Montagu support the argument advanced in the cartoon?
4 How far was Forster's position as expressed in Source C a compromise between the viewpoints expressed in Sources A and B?
5 In what ways did the 1870 Act support voluntary denominational schools?[2]
6 Why was religion such an important issue in the debate over educational reform?[2]

Notes

1 The period was later reduced from a year to six months
2 See text and topic books, for example,
  Read D 1979 *England 1868–1914* Longman, Chap. 6
  Feuchtwanger E J 1985 *Democracy and Empire* Edward Arnold, Chap. 2
  Abbott B H 1972 *Gladstone and Disraeli* Collins, Chap. 3
  Adelman P 1983 *Gladstone, Disraeli and Later Victorian Politics* Longman, 2nd edn, Chap. 1
  Willis M 1989 *Gladstone and Disraeli: Principles and Policies* Cambridge University Press, Chap. 3
  For greater detail see:
  Midwinter E 1970 *Nineteenth Century Education* Longman, Chap. 5

6.3 The 1872 Licensing Act – The Electoral Consequences of Legislation

The Licensing Act restricting public house opening hours became one of the most controversial measures of Gladstone's first ministry. As Liberal defeats mounted in the 1874 General Election, Gladstone observed to a colleague that they had 'been swept away, literally, by a torrent of beer and gin'. To Queen Victoria he wrote that 'the most powerful operative cause' of the defeat was 'the combined and costly action of the publicans except in the North where from their more masculine character the people are not so easily managed'.

The eminent historian, R C K Ensor, supported this interpretation by emphasising the importance of the drink trade in politics and how it went over to the Conservatives following the licensing restrictions in the 1872 Act[1]. More recently Dr Brian Harrison has argued in *Drink and the Victorians* that Ensor's views need modification[2]. There had been much debate over licensing, drunkenness and public order before the Act, and opinions on the measure varied even within parties and interest groups. How far could licensing reform explain the Liberal defeats in the 1874 General Election?

A *When Silas Marner was robbed in George Eliot's novel he immediately thought of reporting the theft at the village inn.*

The Rainbow, in Marner's view, was a place of luxurious resort for rich and stout husbands, whose wives had superfluous stores of linen; it was the place where he was likely to find the powers and dignities of Raveloe, and where he could most speedily make his loss public. He lifted the latch, and turned into the bright bar or kitchen on the right hand, where the less lofty customers of the house were in the habit of assembling, the parlour on the left being reserved for the more select society . . .

Eliot G *Silas Marner* Penguin edn, 1967, pp 94–5
(first published 1861)

B *A Conservative spokesman, Sir Henry Selwin-Ibbetson, speaks on the second reading of the 1872 Bill.*

. . . he hailed the Bill of the Government with the greatest satisfaction . . . He believed that the irregularity of hours was, as regarded the opening and shutting of houses, as injurious as the length of them . . .

. . . As to the shortening of hours, while admitting that the police reports showed that closing at 11 o'clock would be highly beneficial, he could not help feeling that there was another side to the question . . . When public feeling was strong, you lost ground by attempting to go too quickly; it was best to accustom the public by degrees to the benefits resulting from any change . . .

. . . he also regretted that the present Bill, unlike the Suspensory Act of last year, laid down no rule limiting the number of public-houses to the amount of the population of a district . . .

There was nothing he dreaded so much as that a question of this sort should be made a subject of political agitation at an election . . .

Hansard, 11 July 1872. Ser. 3, Vol. 212: 969–74

C *From 'The Brewers' Guardian', 16 July 1872.*

. . . we are strongly of the opinion that this Bill, with a few very trifling amendments . . . is more just and equitable in several important respects to the Trade, whose interests it is our especial duty to consider, than any of the schemes which have been previously introduced, or which, failing the passing of this measure, we are likely to have placed before us in the future . . .

Quoted in Harrison B H 1971 *Drink and the Victorians*
Faber and Faber

D *From the 'Licensed Victuallers' Guardian'.*

The Licensing Act of 1872 has proved injurious alike to the people and to the Trade. It tends to demoralise the former and it destroys the property of the latter . . .

The comforts of the people and the liberty of the subject it totally disregards . . .

The Licensed Victuallers' Guardian, 23 November 1872

E *A report in the 'Licensed Victuallers' Guardian' of a disturbance at Coventry on the Act's enforcement.*

. . . a large concourse of persons assembled in the Broadgate . . . The most favourite song seemed to be, 'Britons never shall be slaves'. Stones were also thrown, several of the police officers being struck. There is in Little Park-street a building used by the City Club, and the cries were raised, 'Down with the City Club', 'Smash the windows', 'Down with the Government', and others of a similar kind . . . For some time the police succeeded in keeping back the mob, but it broke through at last, and rushed to the club . . .

The Licensed Victuallers' Guardian, 31 August 1872

F *From 'The Licensed Victuallers' Gazette'.*

In the last number of the Gazette we printed the division list on the question of the hour for closing public houses on Sunday evenings. As these lists and the votes of the leading members, both Liberal and Conservative, who have recorded their names for the Government or against the public, will be of vast value in future elections as a criterion who are and who are not the licensed victuallers' and people's friends, we subjoin a brief analysis of the leading divisions . . .

Mr Bruce [the Home Secretary responsible for the Bill] moved to add words which would prevent the licensing justices from extending the privileged hours to beerhouses . . . The majority with Ministers included over 40 Conservatives.

The Licensed Victuallers' Gazette, 10 August 1872

G   *From an editorial in 'The Economist'.*

... No Ministry, however strong, and however pressed from the outside by fanatical agitators, would willingly provoke an opposition so formidable as that with which the publican interest threatens every Administration that dares to meddle with the traffic in strong drinks. It is painful and discreditable to be compelled to confess that in so many recent elections the power of 'Beer' has turned the scale, and it is only too probable that whenever Parliament may be dissolved the brewing and distilling interest will command as many votes as ever the old Whig connexion in the palmiest days of close boroughs had under its control ... It turns elections and shakes Administrations, and is courted by parties ... For it must be remembered that Beer was once a great Liberal power, as surely to be reckoned on the Liberal side as Land was to be reckoned on the Conservative side. It is only in our day that the Tories find their safest if not their ablest candidates among the scions of the great brewing and distilling firms.

The Economist, 20 December 1873

Questions

1 How would you account for the difference in opinion between Sources C and D?
2 How far does the evidence in this section suggest that (**a**) class divisions and (**b**) public freedom were important issues in the controversy over the Act?
3 How far do these sources support Gladstone's view that resentment over the Act was 'the most powerful operative cause' of the Liberal government's defeat?
4 How useful are these sources in deciding the electoral importance of the Act and what other evidence would you require to make a judgement?

Notes

1 Ensor R C K 1936 *England 1870–1914* Oxford University Press
2 Harrison B H 1971 *Drink and the Victorians* Faber and Faber. (Much of the evidence in this subsection is cited in this book)

6.4   The 1874 Election – Did Gladstone's First Ministry Fail?

Although not always in government, the Peelites, Whigs and Radicals who came to form the Gladstonian Liberal party had together held a majority in the House of Commons since 1846. For the first time since 1841 the Conservatives won a clear victory in the 1874 General Election. Was this a fair judgement on Gladstone's first ministry?

A   *This extract is taken from a Conservative newspaper, 'The Morning Post'.*

It is impossible to doubt that the result of the elections has given general satisfaction ... The Government have passed three measures with which little fault can be found – the Irish Church and Land Acts, and the Education Act. They may also be credited with the Ballot Act, which has enabled the elections to pass off with comparative quiet; and their Judicature Act ... may also be mentioned in their praise. But in almost every other respect they have failed. Their foreign policy has been mistaken and humiliating. The Abolition of Purchase in the Army by Royal Warrant was offensive both in the matter and the manner of its proceeding ...

These are some of the landmarks of the indiscretion by which the Government has forfeited the confidence of the country, but the catalogue might be easily increased. It is not because the Government has exhausted its programme that the voice of the country has been given against it. It is because with much that has been well done there is still more that has been badly done. But another reason why the elections have left the Government in a minority is that, having done the work for which he was placed in power, the PRIME MINISTER, in order to retain power, has projected more work which the country is determined to oppose. It is totally contrary to the instincts and the habits of Englishmen to be continually indulging in innovations . . .

The Morning Post, 9 February 1874

B *This extract is taken from 'The Economist' which had the previous week described a Conservative government as 'not intrinsically to be desired'.*

. . . being as impartial as we can, our judgment is that the Ministry of Mr Gladstone has had a better combination of great Ministers than any Ministry since the first Reform Act. Some administrations have surpassed it in this or that particular, but, upon the whole, it has done the most and been the best.

. . . There have, indeed been only two Governments of immense power since 1832. The first is the Whig government which followed the Reform Act of that time . . .

The only other Government of similar power since 1832 is that of Sir Robert Peel, which succeeded the election of 1841 . . . but . . . it had no characteristic measures, and is now known by uncharacteristic measures . . .

In this respect the Government of Mr Gladstone is indisputably superior. It has, as everybody admits, been faithful to the principles which it announced. A single mistake in the Education Act is the sole exception which can even be fancied. The Government entered office with a list of congenial measures, and it passed these and others . . .

But, it will be asked, if Mr Gladstone's is so good a Government, why does not the country wish to keep it? We answer that, though a good Government, it has not the particular species of goodness which the public for the moment want. It is in its nature an active and innovating Government, and the country just now wishes a passive and non-innovating Government . . .

The Economist, 14 February 1874

C *These extracts are taken from 'The Liberator', a magazine published by the Nonconformist Liberation Society which aimed at the disestablishment of the Anglican Church.*

But we have also to secure the redress of grievances occasioned by the mistakes of a Government which, until lately, we have earnestly supported, and to prevent that Government going still further astray from, what we deem to be, the line of rectitude in matters ecclesiastical. It has erred in dealing with the Education question . . .

The Liberator, 2 February 1874

The appeal to the constituencies has been made, and the result has been . . . the substitution of a Conservative Government, headed by Mr Disraeli, for the greatest Liberal administration and the most popular Prime Minister of modern times.

. . . it must be acknowledged, that the majority of the population desire rest before undertaking more great organic reforms. Conservatism, also, has become a fashion, rather than a political creed, and the fashion has grown with the growth of the wealthy classes.

The Liberator, 2 March 1874

Questions

1 What do you understand by
  a 'a passive and non-innovating Government' (Source B lines 32–33)?
  b 'the line of rectitude in matters ecclesiastical' (Source C lines 6–7)?
2 Explain why the abolition of purchase in the army was 'offensive both in the matter and the manner of its proceeding' (Source A lines 12–15).[1]
3 How far do the three sources agree on the achievements of Gladstone's ministry?

4 How far do the sources suggest that the election defeat can be explained by:

  a what Disraeli condemned in his election address as the 'incessant and harassing legislation' of Gladstone's first ministry?

  b the failure of Liberal supporters to rally behind the government?

  c social changes outside the government's control?

5 How reliable are the sources in this section as evidence of public opinion in 1874?

Notes

1 See textbooks, for example,
  Feuchtwanger E J 1985 *Democracy and Empire* Edward Arnold, Chap. 2

7 Disraeli's Conservatism

7.1 Was there Substance in Disraeli's Conservatism?

Disraeli was Prime Minister for the first time in 1868 but without a Conservative majority in the House of Commons, and he was soon defeated in the 1868 General Election. There was much criticism of his subsequent performance as Opposition leader, but he reasserted his position in two great speeches in the spring and summer of 1872 which outlined his vision of Conservatism and attacked the current Liberal government. What was the political thinking he outlined and how did contemporaries rate his performance?

A *From Disraeli's speech to Lancashire Conservatives at Manchester, April 1872.*

... the programme of the Conservative party is to maintain the Constitution of the country ... the Constitution of England is not merely a Constitution in State, it is a Constitution in Church and State. The wisest Sovereigns and statesmen have ever been anxious to connect authority with religion ...

... I am not here to maintain that there is nothing to be done to increase the well-being of the working classes of this country, generally speaking. There is not a single class in the country which is not susceptible of improvement ... But in all we do we must remember ... that much depends upon the working classes themselves ... Much also may be expected from that sympathy between classes which is a distinctive feature of the present day; and, in the last place, no inconsiderable results may be obtained by judicious and prudent legislation ...

... I think public attention as regards these matters ought to be concentrated upon sanitary legislation ...

In: Kebbel T E (ed) 1882 *Selected Speeches of the Late Right Hon. the Earl of Beaconsfield*, Vol. II, Longman, pp 491–511

B *From Disraeli's speech to a Conservative banquet at the Crystal Palace, June 1872.*

Now I have always been of opinion that the Tory party has three great objects. The first is to maintain the institutions of the country – not from any sentiment of political superstition, but because we believe that they embody the principles upon which a community like England can alone safely rest ...

Gentlemen, there is another and second great object of the Tory party ... to uphold the Empire of England ...

Gentlemen, another great object of the Tory party, and one not inferior to the maintenance of the Empire, or the upholding of our institutions, is the elevation of the condition of the people ... ... the views which I expressed in the great capital of the county of Lancaster have been held up to derision by the Liberal Press. A leading member – a very rising member, at least, among the new Liberal members – denounced them the other day as the 'policy of sewage.'

Well, it may be the 'policy of sewage' to a Liberal member of Parliament. But to one of the labouring multitude of England, who has found fever always to be one of the inmates of his household – who has, year after year, seen stricken down the children of his loins, on whose sympathy and material support he has looked with hope and confidence, it is not a 'policy of sewage,' but a question of life and death . . .

Why, the people of England would be greater idiots than the Jacobinical leaders[1] of London even suppose, if, with their experience and acuteness, they should not long have seen that the time had arrived when social, and not political improvement is the object which they ought to pursue . . . I find a rising opinion in the country sympathising with our tenets, and prepared, I believe, if the opportunity offers, to uphold them until they prevail . . .

Upon you depends the issue . . . You have nothing to trust to but your own energy and the sublime instinct of an ancient people . . .

In: Kebbel T E (ed) 1882 *Selected Speeches of the Late Right Hon. the Earl of Beaconsfield*, Vol. II, Longman, pp 525–35

C   *'The Times' comments on Disraeli's speech in Manchester.*

. . . those who asked themselves beforehand whether Mr DISRAELI would have a policy to unfold at Manchester and came to the conclusion that he would not may plume themselves on their foresight. The speech may be described with great and equal justice as witty or didactic, as odd or original, as paradoxical or profound. Further, it must be allowed that no other man could have spoken at such length and have been so diverting throughout. But when we search for the positive policy of the next Conservative Government, all we can find is that it will pay the closest attention to sanitary legislation . . .

The Times, 4 April 1872

D   *This extract is taken from the private diary of a Conservative leader, Gathorne Hardy.*

. . . Disraeli's speech very long & in parts very good. No programme, as how could there be? His reception Wilson Patten says was beyond anything he ever saw.

In: Johnson N E (ed) 1981 *The Diary of Gathorne Hardy, later Lord Cranbrook, 1866–1892: Political Selections* Oxford University Press, p 154

E *A cartoon from 'Punch', 6 July 1872, commenting on Disraeli's speech at the Crystal Palace.*

THE CONSERVATIVE PROGRAMME.

"DEPUTATION BELOW, SIR.—WANT TO KNOW THE CONSERVATIVE PROGRAMME."

Rt. Hon. Ben. Diz. "EH?—OH!—AH!—YES!—QUITE SO! TELL THEM, MY GOOD ABERCORN, WITH MY COMPLIMENTS, THAT WE PROPOSE TO RELY ON THE SUBLIME INSTINCTS OF AN ANCIENT PEOPLE!!"

F *An attack on Disraeli by the Liberal minister, Robert Lowe[2], at the 1874 General Election.*

... he is not accustomed to look at facts when he is making an estimate. The other day he said he left the Income-tax at 4d. Yes, but I found it at 6d ... He has a sort of harum-scarum, splatter-dash, inaccurate, careless way of dealing with things which makes him utterly unfit to be the ruler of such a nation ...

The Times, 4 February 1874

G *A comment from 'The Economist'.*

Mr Lowe ... undoubtedly proved that [Disraeli] had a most inaccurate mind, that he was sure to make some mistake of fact about every ten sentences, and that if the office of Premier were subjected to the Civil Service Commissioners, the Conservative leader would be plucked to a certainty. But there is much of life that Civil Service Commissioners cannot test ... Mr Disraeli is at least a great man of the world; he has watched the vanities, and can appreciate the motives, of human nature; he has also a cool, impartial mind; and these are valuable ingredients in a Premier's character, and will tend to counterbalance even the most flagrant degree of inaccuracy ...

The Economist, 7 February 1874

H *Disraeli's Home Secretary, Richard Cross, describes a Cabinet meeting after the Conservative victory at the 1874 General Election in a memoir privately published in 1903.*

When the Cabinet came to discuss the Queen's speech, I was, I confess, disappointed at the want of originality shown by the Prime Minister. From all his speeches, I had quite expected that his mind was full of legislative schemes, but such did not prove to be the case; on the contrary, he had to entirely rely on the various suggestions of his colleagues, and as they themselves had only just come into office, and that suddenly, there was some difficulty in framing the Queen's speech.

Viscount Cross 1903 'A Political History', p 25. In: Smith P 1967 *Disraelian Conservatism and Social Reform* Routledge and Kegan Paul, p 199

Questions

1 What do you understand by 'the institutions of the country' (Source B line 3)?
2 What do Sources A and B suggest about the importance Disraeli attached to social legislation and his reasons for advocating it?
3 Sources C, D, E, F and H are very different types of sources all commenting on the substance and precision of Disraeli's speeches and political thinking. How useful are they as indications of opinion among the public and politicians and as judgements on Disraeli's thinking and oratory?
4 Using all the sources in this section, how substantial do you think Disraeli's political thinking was in the 1870s? Consider how far he had distinctive and well worked out political beliefs, an understanding of contemporary society or a programme for action on specific problems.
5 With reference to section 4.2, how far do you think Disraeli's Conservatism was similar to that of earlier Conservative thinkers and leaders?
6 How far does Disraeli's record as Prime Minister support the judgement of *The Economist* in Source G?[3]

Notes

1 'Jacobinical leaders' – left-wing leaders advocating the kind of policies which the ex-

tremist Jacobins had put forward and implemented during the most advanced stages of the French Revolution

2 Robert Lowe was the Chancellor of the Exchequer in the Liberal government which took over from Disraeli's first ministry in 1868

3 For this and the next section see text and topic books, for example,
Feuchtwanger E J 1985 *Democracy and Empire* Edward Arnold, Chap. 3
Abbott B H 1972 *Gladstone and Disraeli* Collins
Adelman P 1983 *Gladstone, Disraeli and Later Victorian Politics* Longman, 2nd edn
Coleman B 1988 *Conservatism and the Conservative Party in Nineteenth-Century Britain* Edward Arnold, Chap. 5
The authoritative biography of Disraeli is:
Blake R 1966 *Disraeli* Eyre and Spottiswoode
A full examination of social policy is given in:
Smith P 1967 *Disraelian Conservatism and Social Reform* Routledge and Kegan Paul

7.2 Conservative Social Reform – The Achievement of the Artisans Dwelling Act

One of the best-known pieces of social legislation in Disraeli's second ministry was the Artisans Dwelling Act introduced by R A Cross in 1875 to encourage the removal of rookeries – urban slum areas. What were his aims? What did the Act achieve and how far does it indicate that Disraeli's government was a ministry of social reform?

A *Cross reviews the Act in his memoirs.*

Taking it as a starting point that, apart from the due administration of the Poor Law, it is not the duty of the State to provide any class of citizens with any of the necessaries of life ... but that, at the same time, it is the right and duty of the State to interfere in matters relating to sanitary laws ... I brought in and

carried a Bill to enable local authorities to buy up the old rookeries and rebuild ... Though much remains still to be done, all the really large old rookeries in London were swept away under this Act.

Viscount Cross, A Political History 1868–1900, privately published 1903, pp 33–4

B *From the Artisans Dwelling Act, 1875.*

Where an official representation as hereinafter mentioned is made to the local authority [in London and urban sanitary districts with over 25,000 population] that any houses, courts, or alleys within a certain area under the jurisdiction of the local authority are unfit for human habitation, or that diseases indicating a generally low condition of health amongst the population have been from time to time prevalent in a certain area within the jurisdiction of the local authority, and that such prevalence may reasonably be attributed to the closeness, narrowness, and bad arrangement or the bad condition of the streets and houses or groups of houses within such area ... the local authority shall take such representation into their consideration, and if satisfied of the truth thereof, and of the sufficiency of their resources, shall pass a resolution to the effect that such area is an unhealthy area, and that an improvement scheme ought to be made in respect of such area, and after passing such resolution, they shall forthwith proceed to make a scheme for the improvement of such area.

Act for Facilitating the Improvement of the Dwellings of the Working Classes in Large Towns, 1875, Part 1, Clause 3. In: Handcock W D (ed) 1977 English Historical Documents 1874–1914 Eyre and Spottiswoode, p 615

C *From a book by the Liberal P W Clayden attacking Disraeli's ministry and published before the 1880 General Election.*

[The Artisans Dwelling Act] was, in reality, a Liberal legacy. Mr Torrens[1] had carried a measure in 1866[2] which would have enabled local authorities to remove unwholesome dwellings; but Lord Westbury cut it down in the House of Lords by leaving out the clauses which empowered those authorities to give compensation to owners whose property was condemned; and in consequence, the Act was never carried out. In the Session of 1874, Mr U Kay Shuttleworth[3] had proposed a resolution declaring that 'a necessity exists for some measure that will provide for the improvement of the poorest classes of dwellings in London, and that this question demands the early attention of Her Majesty's Government' ... Mr Cross's Artisan's Dwelling Bill was brought in as a consequence of this expression of Parliamentary opinion. Mr Cross described it as a Bill for the suppression of rookeries; but the suppression takes place to the great profit of the owners of the rookeries and the great loss of the ratepayers ...

> Clayden P W 1880 *England under Lord Beaconsfield*
> Kegan Paul, p 125

D *From a report of the Charity Organisation Society on the operation of the Act to the end of 1879.*

[In London] Action is being taken regarding 1,402 houses. Areas comprising 945 houses and 6 acres have been sold and dealt with ... There are, besides the Metropolis, 87 towns in England and Wales to which the Act is applicable. Out of these one – Birmingham – is dealing with an area of 93 acres, at an estimated cost of £1,310,000 ... In 77 towns no steps whatever have been taken. In no provincial town have the transactions under the Act actually been completed ...

> *Dwellings of the Poor*, Report of the Charity
> Organisation Society, 1881, p 17

Questions

1 Why did the Artisans Dwelling Act operate to 'the great profit of the owners of the rookeries and the great loss of the ratepayers' (Source C lines 22–24)?

2 With reference to Sources A and B explain in what ways the Artisans Dwelling Act was a piece of 'permissive legislation'.

3 Why do you think Cross maintained that it was 'not the duty of the State to provide any class of citizens with any of the necessaries of life' (Source A lines 3–4)?

4 Sources A, C and D contain very varying types of assessment of the Artisans Dwelling Act. With reference to the authors, their motives and the date of writing consider how useful each of these is to the historian.

5 How far does Disraeli's second ministry deserve credit for the Artisans Dwelling Act? Consider the terms of the Act, how far it was a practical measure and what was achieved under it. To what extent were Conservative ministers or others responsible for the ideas behind it, its drafting and its passage into law?[4]

Notes

1 Torrens was a Liberal MP
2 Torrens' bill was passed in 1868, and not 1866 as Clayden states
3 Kay Shuttleworth was a Liberal MP
4 See reading references in section 7.1

7.3 'Beaconsfieldism' in Action: The Zulu War

In the later years of Disraeli's government Gladstone launched a sustained attack on 'Beaconsfieldism' – the name used by Liberal opponents for the ministry's imperial policy which involved extension and consolidation of colonial frontiers.

The problems this brought are well illustrated in the Zulu War which the British fought in South Africa in 1879. Disraeli's Colonial Secretary, Lord Caernarvon, aimed to join colonies of English and former Dutch settlers into one British-controlled federation which would help secure the strategically important Cape Colony and increase Britain's influence in the area. The annexation of the Transvaal in 1877 was in line with this policy, and the Governor of Cape Colony, Sir Bartle Frere, was also particularly keen to extend British control. Sir Michael Hicks Beach who replaced Caernarvon in February 1878 did little to curb Frere's ambitions until October when the government grew increasingly concerned about its military commitments. Events then moved rapidly towards the Zulu War of 1879 in which a British force under Lord Chelmsford was defeated at Isandhlwana. Victory was eventually achieved, but at a considerable cost in money, lives and military prestige. How far were government ambitions and mismanagement to blame?

A *Sir Bartle Frere explains his fears about the Zulus in a letter to Hicks Beach, 30 September 1878.*

The Zulus are now quite out of hand, and the maintenance of peace depends on their forbearance ...

I speak with a deep sense of responsibility for what I say, when I assure you that the peace of South Africa for many years to come seems to me to depend on your taking steps to put a final end to Zulu pretensions to dictate to Her Majesty's Government what they may or may not do to protect Her Majesty's Colonies in South Africa, and that unless you settle with the Zulus, you will find it difficult, if not impossible, to govern the Transvaal without a considerable standing force of Her Majesty's troops.

Martineau J 1895 *The Life of Sir Bartle Frere*, Vol. II, John Murray, pp 244–5

B *Hicks Beach writes to Disraeli, 3 November 1878.*

I cannot really control [Sir B Frere] without a telegraph – (I don't know that I could with one) – I feel it is as likely as not that he is at war with the Zulus at the present moment; and if his forces should prove inadequate, or the Transvaal Boers should take the opportunity to rise, he will be in a great difficulty, and we shall be blamed for not supporting him.

Hicks Beach V 1932 *Life of Sir Michael Hicks Beach*, Vol. I, Macmillan, p 103

C *Following Cabinet discussion, Hicks Beach writes to Frere on 7 November 1878. Frere received the letter on 13 December, but a telegraphed summary had reached him on 30 November.*

... though I hope by this time the 'special service officers' are on their way ... yet the Government are not prepared to comply with the request for more troops. The fact is, that matters in Eastern Europe and India, of which you have by this time heard, wear so serious an aspect that *we cannot now have a Zulu war in addition to other greater and too possible troubles.* When the intelligence of these difficulties reaches you, I have no doubt that you will at once divine the situation – and will redouble the exertions which I am sure you have already employed to avoid the outbreak of any such war, as from your despatch of Sept. 30 I fear you thought too probable at the date at which it was written.

Hicks Beach V 1932 *Life of Sir Michael Hicks Beach*, Vol. I, p 104

D   *On 8 December 1878 Frere sent the Zulu chief Cetywayo an ultimatum demanding major changes in the Zulu military and social system. Frere writes to Hicks Beach about the ultimatum on 23 December 1878.*

My own impression is that it is quite impossible for Cetywayo to submit without calling in our aid to coerce the Frankenstein he has created in his regular regiments. Even if he were sincere and convinced of our superior power – neither of which I believe – he would find a large residuum of his soldiers who are fully convinced of their own superiority to us and will not give in without a trial of strength. I judge from the almost universal impression I find among natives out of Zululand that the natives are the stronger power and will beat the English. Cetywayo may promise anything to get rid of Lord Chelmsford and his troops, but that he will perform what is necessary for our security I do not believe, and we prepare accordingly.

Martineau J 1895 *The Life of Sir Bartle Frere*, Vol. II, John Murray, p 263

E   *Hicks Beach responds to the ultimatum in a dispatch to Frere, 23 January 1879.*

In order to afford protection to the lives and property of the Colonists the reinforcements asked for were supplied, and in informing you of the decision of Her Majesty's Government, I took the opportunity of impressing upon you the importance of using every effort to avoid war. But the terms which you have dictated to the Zulu king, however necessary to relieve the Colony in future from an impending and increasing danger, are evidently such as he may not improbably refuse, even at the risk of war; and I regret that the necessity for immediate action should have appeared to you so imperative as to preclude you from incurring the delay which would have been involved in consulting Her Majesty's Government upon a subject of so much importance as

the terms which Cetywayo should be required to accept, before those terms were actually presented to the Zulu king.

In making these observations however, I do not desire to question the propriety of the policy which you have adopted in the face of a difficult and complicated condition of affairs . . .

. . . I sincerely trust that the policy you have adopted may be as successful as the very careful consideration which you have given to it deserves, and that, if military operations should become necessary, . . . they should be brought to an early and decisive termination . . .

PRO Colonial Office Papers 48 487.

F   *Following serious losses in the Zulu War, Hicks Beach gives Frere a government reprimand in a dispatch sent on 19 March 1879 and subsequently published.*

[H.M. Government] have been unable to find in the documents you have placed before them that evidence of urgent necessity for immediate action which alone could justify you in taking, without their full knowledge and sanction, a course almost certain to result in a war, which, as I had previously impressed upon you, every effort should have been used to avoid.

. . . They cannot, however, doubt that your further action will be such as to prevent a recurrence of any cause for complaint on this score; and they have no desire to withdraw, in the present crisis of affairs, the confidence hitherto reposed in you, the continuance of which is now more than ever needed to conduct our difficulties in South Africa to a successful termination.

Correspondence respecting the affairs of South Africa, p 109. *Parliamentary Papers 1878–79*, Vol. LIII

G *From a private letter Disraeli wrote to Lady Chesterfield, 28 June 1879.*

... Sir Bartle Frere, who ought to be impeached[1], writes always as if he were quite unconscious of having done anything wrong!

Marquis of Zetland (ed) *The Letters of Disraeli to Lady Bradford and Lady Chesterfield*, Vol. II, Ernest Benn, p 225

H *Gladstone condemns the Zulu War in a speech during his famous by-election campaign in Midlothian, November 1879.*

If we cast our eyes to South Africa, what do we behold? That a nation whom we term savages have in defence of their own land offered their naked bodies to the terribly improved artillery and arms of modern European science, and have been mowed down by hundreds and by thousands, having committed no offence, but having, with rude and ignorant courage, done what were for them, and done faithfully and bravely what were for them, the duties of patriotism ...

Gladstone W E 1880 *Political Speeches in Scotland*, Vol. I, A Elliot, pp 90–1

Questions

1 What do Sources A, C and H suggest were the main concerns of (**a**) Sir Bartle Frere (**b**) the government and (**c**) Gladstone in deciding what should and what should not be done in South Africa in 1878–79?

2 With reference to Sources B–G do you think Frere disobeyed government orders? How far did the considerations outlined in Source A justify his conduct?

3 Using Sources A–E how far do you think the government should be held responsible for the early defeats and losses in the Zulu War?

4 What judgements did the government make on Frere's past and future conduct in Source F? How far do you think this dispatch was justifiable? What alternative courses could the government have taken and what action would you have decided on in Disraeli's position?

Notes

1 Impeached – brought to trial by Parliament

8 Ireland

8.1 The Impact of the Famine

English rulers had asserted rights over Ireland since 1171 when Henry II claimed the lordship of the island. In the sixteenth century, England gained a more effective control under Elizabeth I, and centuries of tension followed between the Celtic Irish and their English government.

From 1845 to 1849 a catastrophic famine hit the Irish people who had represented 30% of the United Kingdom's population in the 1841 census. Its economic effects were clearly profound, but what were the human and political implications? Ireland had lost its own Parliament less than half a century before and many Irish people felt that they were being governed by an alien administration. How adequate and justifiable was the British government's response to the crisis and how did the Famine alter Ireland's relations with her foreign rulers?

A *Census figures for the Irish population 1821–51.*

	Total population (thousands)	Per cent increase or decrease over 10-year period
1821	6802	
1831	7767	+ 14.19
1841	8175	+ 5.25
1851	6552	− 19.85

Figures from: Mitchell B R, Deane P 1971 *Abstract of British Historical Statistics* Cambridge University Press, p 7

B *From a letter written by George Dawson, an Irish landowner in January 1847.*

I can think of nothing else than the wretched condition of this wretched people. We are comparatively well off in this neighbourhood. There is not want of food; but it is at such a price, as to make it totally impossible for a poor man to support his family with the wages he receives. I do not exaggerate when I tell you that from the moment I open my hall door in the morning until dark, I have a crowd of women and children crying out for something to save them from starving. The men, except the old and infirm, stay away and show the greatest patience and resignation. I have been obliged to turn my kitchen into a bakery and soup shop to enable me to feed the miserable children and mothers that cannot be sent away empty. So great is their distress that they actually faint on getting food into their stomachs. The only reply to my question of 'What do you want?' is, 'I want something to eat', is so simple, so universal, that it tells its own tale, and neither rags nor sickness nor worn out faces or emaciated limbs can make their situation more truly pitiable than these few words . . .

In: *The Great Famine* The Public Record Office of Northern Ireland

C *A funeral at Skibbereen, County Cork.*

[COUNTRY EDITION.]

THE FAMINE IN IRELAND.—FUNERAL AT SKIBBEREEN.—FROM A SKETCH BY MR. H. SMITH, CORK.

The Illustrated London News, 30 January 1847

D *In the twentieth century a woman at Sneem, County Kerry remembered her uncle's story about the suffering of a family called Casey at the time of the famine.*

There were seven or eight of them, a neat little family; they had white heads. My uncle Mick used to cry when he used be telling the story. The oldest girl went six days of the week to Sneem for soup and came empty. On the seventh day five of them died. I remembered one of them [a survivor] – she was a withered old little woman ... The 'ologon' [noise] they ruz [raised] the sixth day, when she came without any food was something dreadful. Years after, my father was ditching near the ruin and he found the bones of an old man and a child; the arm of the old man was around the child.

In: Edwards R D, Williams T D 1956 *The Great Famine* Browne and Nolan, pp 420–1

E *The Prime Minister, Lord John Russell announces famine relief measures in Parliament.*

... I wish ... to declare, that we cannot expect, and that we do not expect, to be able by any measures which the Government, or by any measures which Parliament may adopt, to ward off or prevent the effects of the awful visitation under which Ireland is suffering. It is not in the power of man to do away with the effects of such a calamity ... I am astonished that, at a time of famine, men of education ... should tell [the Irish people] that they were to demand from Parliament 'such steps as may insure an immediate, constant, and cheap supply of food.' Why, Sir, this is a task which is impossible for us – a task which they ought to tell their countrymen the destitution under which they are suffering has made impossible for man – a task which is beyond all human power; and that all that we can possibly do is in some measure to alleviate the existing distress ...

... Let me say ... that I think, that although, unhappily, we have been diverted from the observance of general principles with respect to these matters, yet I do think that we ought to observe general principles as far as possible, and that these general principles prescribe thus much with respect to the interference of the Government. That interference may be given in three ways, and these three ways ought, as far as possible, to be kept separate and distinct. First, the Government, with the support of Parliament, may grant assistance to individual proprietors for the purpose of enabling them to improve their private properties. Secondly, it may assist them in public works by making roads, or partly by grants in aid of public works, which are evidently of public utility. And thirdly, it may enact that relief should be given by law to the destitute.

... there are some things which the Crown cannot grant, which Parliament cannot enact – these are the spirit of self-reliance and the spirit of co-operation ... happy will it be, indeed, if the Irish themselves take for their maxim, ''Help yourselves and Heaven will help you;'' and then I trust they will find there have been some ''uses in adversity'' ...

Hansard, 25 January 1847. Ser. 3, Vol. 89: 438–52

F *Many Irish people emigrated to North America during the famine. This is the start of the 'Address of the Massachusetts Irish Emigrant Aid Society to Irishmen in the United States' published in 1855.*

FELLOW COUNTRYMEN:
The time has at length arrived for action. Every steamer that crosses the Atlantic, to our shores, brings intelligence of fresh disasters, distress, and difficulty to our old inveterate foe. Let us therefore unite in a bond of brotherhood to aid the cause of Liberty for Ireland.

The moment is propitious – the means are in our hands. Let us use them – use them with prudence, with caution; but with devoted energy and the determination of men, whose birthright is a heritage of vengeance – vengeance of seven centuries of wrong, of massacre, of spoliation, of rapine, of tyranny, deceit and treachery, unparalleled in the annals of the world's history.

... remember the long, bitter years of exile, and think of that beautiful land, the home of your childhood and affections; where repose the ashes of your fathers, and the martyrs of your race; and say, shall no effort be made to wrest the Island from the Robber Pirate who has so long held her in the grip of tyranny, depressed the energies of her people, and despoiled them of their inheritance?

Citizen, II, 25 August 1855. In: Abbott E (ed) 1926 *Historical Aspects of the Immigration Problem: Select Documents* University of Chicago Press, pp 475–6

Questions

1 How far do the figures in Source A suggest that the famine produced a change in trend in Irish population?

2 **a** What were the 'fresh disasters, distress, and difficulty to our old inveterate foe' (Source F lines 4–6)?

b To what 'general principles' was Russell referring (Source E line 23)?

3 How usable is Source C as an indication of suffering in the famine?

4 How far and in what ways is oral evidence of the past such as that in Source D useful to the historian?

5 How far do Sources B and D and the evidence in section 4.4 support Russell's argument that the task of ensuring 'an immediate, constant, and cheap supply of food' in Ireland was 'beyond all human power' (Source E lines 12–13, 18).

6 What famine relief measures did British governments take in 1845–49 and how prompt and effective were they?

7 How far did the suffering caused by the famine worsen relations between the British government and the Irish people and how might the consequences make future British government of Ireland more difficult?

Notes

1 For this and later sections in this chapter, see:
Morton G 1980 *Home Rule and the Irish Question*
Longman
For more detailed accounts, see:
Beckett J C 1966 *The Making of Modern Ireland 1603–1923* Faber and Faber
Lyons F S L 1973 *Ireland since the Famine* Fontana
Foster R F 1988 *Modern Ireland 1600–1972* Allen Lane

8.2 A Liberal Approach to Ireland: Gladstone's Second Land Act

Most of Ireland's agricultural land was owned by landlords whose powers to raise rents and evict tenants became major grievances among the country's farmers. Gladstone, who was deeply concerned with Irish affairs, attempted to tackle the problem in his first Land Act of 1870, but the act, which generally respected property rights and underwent modification in the House of Lords, failed to satisfy tenant farmers. With severe agricultural depression at the end of the 1870s there was a great increase in agrarian crime and unrest so that Gladstone faced a violent, troubled Ireland at the start of his second ministry in 1880. His second Land Act of 1881 was an attempt to settle the land question. Did it fail?

A *Gladstone introduces his Land Bill in the House of Commons.*

On the morning that this Bill passes every landlord and tenant will be subject to certain new provisions of the law of great importance. In the first place, an increase of rent will be restrained by certain rules. In the second place, the compensation for disturbance will be regulated according to different rates. And in the third place – more important probably than any – the right to sell the tenant's interest will be universally established. These are some of the means outside the Court which we propose; but there will also remain to the tenant the full power of going to the Court to fix a judicial rent, which may be followed by judicial tenant right. The judicial rent will entail a statutory term of 15 years ... Evictions will hereafter, we trust, be only for default ...

Hansard, 7 April 1881. Ser. 3, Vol. 260: 923

B *The Cowper Report reviews its effects in 1887.*

The number of agricultural holders of land in Ireland according to the census return of 1881 was 499,108 ... It has been roughly estimated that about 150,000 of the total number were leaseholders. All leases were excepted from the operation of the Land Act of 1881 ... After deducting leaseholders there were left, in round numbers, about 350,000 holders of land, the great majority of whom held as tenants from year to year ...

... After the judicial rent has been fixed the tenant is practically entitled to hold his farm without disturbance for an unlimited period, provided he observes the statutable conditions, which include the payment of the fixed rent ...

The grievances to which tenants were liable by reason of insecurity of tenure were thus entirely removed by the provisions of the Land Act of 1881 ...

The entire number of fair rents fixed by all the methods provided by the Act between the 21st of August 1881 and the 22nd of August 1886 was 176,800. The leaseholders are as yet excepted, but ... after making a large allowance for other excepted holdings, we arrive at the conclusion that about 150,000 tenants who were entitled to avail themselves of the provisions of the Land Act of 1881 have not yet done so ...

... In all, by the operation of the Act, including arbitrations, a rental of 3,227,021l. has been reduced to 2,638,549l., a per-centage reduction of 18.2 ...

The fall in the price of produce of all kinds, and in all parts of the country, has much impaired the ability of the farmers to pay the full rent. And this, following on a previous general restriction of credit by the banks and other lenders of money, as well as by the shop-keepers, has very greatly increased their financial difficulties . . .

Report of the Royal Commission on the Land Law (Ireland) Act, 1881, and the Purchase of Land (Ireland) Act, 1885, pp 5–8. *Parliamentary Papers 1887,* Vol. XXVI

C *Michael Davitt, the founder of the Land League, which led agrarian agitation in 1879–82, comments on the operation of the act.*

The state was virtually to supplant the landlord. He was to be reduced to the position of an annuitant, but still carrying in his maimed position as a landlord enough of the odium attaching to an evil system to keep Celtic hatred of it alive and active, and offering new incentives for continued destructive agitation in a partisan administration of the new land law. For what happened was this: Mr Gladstone gave the potential benefits of the new system to the tenants of Ireland, while Dublin Castle invested the interpretation and administration of the land act in the landlords and their nominees. It was England's traditional way of spoiling the value and of marring the efficacy of a peace-making reform . . . The principle of the Land Law Act is that a fair, judicial rent is not to include the value of improvements made by the tenants or his predecessors . . .

In practice there is no presumption that existing improvements are the tenant's, for he must claim beforehand in writing such improvements as he can prove by strictly legal evidence – by witnesses who have seen the work performed – and only gets credit for such improvements as he does so prove . . .

These and many other subterfuges of a similar kind were the legal machinery created and applied by landlord influence in Dublin Castle and in Irish courts to deprive the tenants of the full benefits of Mr Gladstone's great measure . . .

Davitt M 1904 *The Fall of Feudalism in Ireland* Harper and Bros, pp 321–3

Questions

1 What do you understand by
   a 'Evictions will . . . be only for default' (Source A lines 16–18)?
   b 'the landlord . . . reduced to the position of an annuitant' (Source C lines 1–3)?
   c 'Dublin Castle' (Source C lines 11–12, 30)?
2 Which three major rights does Gladstone promise tenants under the act in Source A? How far would these lead to the state virtually supplanting the landlord as Davitt suggests in Source C?
3 How far do Sources B and C suggest that the continuing problems over Irish land tenure were due to the terms of the act, its application or changing economic conditions?
4 Compare the conclusions in Sources B and C about the success of the act in achieving Gladstone's aims and the reasons for its partial failure. How would you account for any differences?

8.3 A Conservative Approach – 'Bloody' Balfour and Land Purchase

In the years following 1881 Gladstone became convinced that no measures of reform would reconcile the Irish to English administration. In 1886 he therefore introduced a Home Rule Bill to give the Irish limited self-government. This was accompanied by a large-scale land purchase scheme involving government loans which would enable Irish tenants to buy their holdings from the landlords. Gladstone subsequently had to drop the land purchase scheme, and his Home Rule Bill was defeated, splitting the Liberal Party and leading to several years of Conservative government under Lord Salisbury. Salisbury's surprise choice as Chief Secretary for Ireland was his nephew Arthur Balfour who faced growing unrest which included the Mitchelstown massacre soon after his appointment in 1887. But he was responsible, first as Irish Secretary and later as Prime Minister, for measures to improve the prosperity of the Irish countryside that included important land purchase acts.

A *Balfour outlines his policy as Chief Secretary for Ireland.*

Cromwell failed because he relied solely upon repressive measures. That mistake I shall not imitate. I shall be as relentless as Cromwell in enforcing obedience to the law, but, at the same time, I shall be as radical as any reformer in redressing grievances, and especially in removing every cause of complaint in regard to the land. It is on the twofold aspect of my policy that I rely for success. Hitherto, English Governments have stood first upon one leg and then upon the other. They have either been all for repression, or all for reform. I am for both; repression as stern as Cromwell: reform as thorough as Mr Parnell or anyone else can desire.

In: Alderson B 1903 *Arthur James Balfour: The Man and his Work* Grant Richards, p 71

B *From a report in 'The Times' of violence at a meeting in Mitchelstown when police tried to force their way through a large crowd so that a government shorthand writer could take notes on the speeches.*

... The head constable in charge of the men drew his bayonet, but the crowd assumed a very threatening attitude, and the note-taker could not get in. A large force of police numbering about 40, then came up and tried to make an entrance, but they were met by the crowd with sticks and stones. The men, formed into a solid square, tried without firing to keep back the crowd. They were subjected, however, to unmerciful treatment, several men being severely injured. They retreated, and when they arrived at the barracks they fired several shots to keep back the crowd. The barracks were besieged with stones, and the police were obliged to come out and fire on the crowd. Having been reinforced they sallied out into the street and charged the crowd. A volley was fired and two men were shot, one on the centre of the square, and the other at the corner ...

The Times, 10 September 1887

C *An Irish newspaper 'The Freeman's Journal' reports the Mitchelstown fighting.*

... there was then a squad of fifty policemen on the outskirts of the meeting trying to force their way in ... In an instant all was confusion ...

Never in some considerable experience have I ever seen the police so faced before. I have been accustomed to see police ... baton and bayonet women and children, and it was impossible to shed a tear when seeing them opposed by men who handled the stick as well as the best of them. The countrymen stood together and fought the police foot to foot amid a tempest of shouts and cheers ...

From a later dispatch on the same day:

... I regret to say that two deaths have already taken place as a result of the mad police fusilade ...

The Freeman's Journal, 10 September 1887

D *Balfour supports the police action.*

... when you are dealing with police or soldiers, you cannot expect absolute accuracy of aim; and it is impossible to say, if the order to fire is once given, who will be the victims.

That, no doubt, is a conclusive reason for deferring to the last dread necessity the act of firing. It has never been a reason, and, if I have my way, it never will be a reason, for not firing when self-defence and the authority of the law actually require it ... if [*The Freeman's Journal* account] be accurate, or anything like accurate, the conduct of the police stands out absolutely justifiable ...

Hansard, 12 September 1887. Ser. 3, Vol. 321: 326–7

E   *Balfour outlines his policy on land reform when supporting his government's Land Purchase Bill as Prime Minister in 1903.*

In 1881 Mr Gladstone carried out to its extreme issue the policy inaugurated in 1870 with regard to Irish land. The principle of free contract as between landlord and tenant, which was altered by the Act of 1870, was in 1881 wholly destroyed ... the Act of 1881 was passed against the strong feeling and the vehement criticism of the Party to which I belong; and we, or some of us, saw that the only possible way of bringing these evils to an end was by promoting land purchase, and that the only way to promote land purchase effectually was to employ the credit of the State to carry out that great national object ... ... Ever since the great land difficulties in Ireland arose, ever since 1881, and explicitly since 1883 it has been the policy of the Unionist Party to substitute by land purchase a system of single ownership for that system of dual ownership established in 1881, under peculiar circumstances, but having within it the seeds of failure, seeds which have borne an abundant and most dangerous harvest ...

... the Bill is not intended to make people loyal. I admit that. It is not intended to turn Home Rulers into Unionists. I admit that. But it is intended to take away one of those sores which fester and which aggravate every political movement which might otherwise be innocuous ... Emotions which are the result of long generations of ancient and bitter traditions are not easy to blot out ... We think that good government and contentment ought to end and will end, ought to tend and will tend – I will put it in that more moderate

form – to a harmony of feeling between every section of the community, whether in Ireland, Scotland, or England. But the primary object of this measure is to substitute a good system of land tenure for a bad system, and to remove some of those intolerable absurdities ... which resulted in making the Irish land laws a chaos and a by-word ...

Hansard, 4 May 1903. Ser. 4, Vol. 121: 1243–55

Questions

1 What do you understand by
   a 'repression as stern as Cromwell' (Source A line 13)?
   b 'reform as thorough as Mr Parnell' could desire (Source A lines 13–15)?
   c 'the policy inaugurated in 1870' (Source E line 2)?
2 Compare the sympathies displayed in Sources B and C and the accounts they give of events at Mitchelstown.
3 What criticisms does Balfour make of Liberal legislation and how far does he suggest a different policy from Gladstone's in Source E?
4 With reference to the sources in this section and your own knowledge examine how far Balfour combined policies of repression and reform as he intended in Source A.
5 How extensive were the land purchases made under the 1903 Act? How far did the Conservative land and rural development reforms help to produce 'contentment' and 'harmony of feeling' as Balfour hoped?[1]

Notes

1 In addition to earlier references, see:
Winstanley M J 1984 *Ireland and the Land Question 1800–1922* Methuen
Hoppen K T 'Making things more complicated: Politics and agrarianism in modern Ireland.' *History* June 1988

8.4 The Twentieth-Century Debate Over Home Rule

From 1886 the Liberal party was committed to granting Ireland the limited self-government known as Home Rule, but later Liberal leaders did not share Gladstone's passionate attachment to the reform. The Irish, therefore, gained little from the Liberal government elected in 1906, but when the Liberals lost their overall majority in the general elections of 1910, Irish Nationalist MPs led by John Redmond offered the government support at a price – Home Rule.

Since it appeared as a serious political possibility in 1886 there had also been significant Irish opposition to Home Rule concentrated in Ulster whose substantial Protestant population feared domination by the Roman Catholic majority. In the crisis from 1910 Ulstermen found a leader of national standing in Sir Edward Carson who led Irish Unionist opposition to the Home Rule Bill introduced by Asquith's Liberal government in 1912. The following extracts came from Redmond's and Carson's speeches in the Parliamentary debates on the bill.

A *John Redmond.*

The principle of devolving on local assemblies the management of local affairs has at its back the sanction of the whole world. It has at its back the sanction of the Empire. Why, it is the foundation of the Empire to-day, and it is the bond, and the only bond, of union. I think it is true to say that no community of white men within the Empire has ever asked for this right, and up to this has been refused the exercise of it . . .

Hansard, 11 April 1912. Ser. 5, Vol. 36: 1443

B *Sir Edward Carson.*

. . . Has there ever in the whole of the history of our country been any precedent to which you can point for turning out a great community, successful under your rule, cleaving to your rule and desiring to remain under it, because other people have been discontented and say that they have failed to work successfully under your rule?

Take the four counties alone . . . which, I believe, are referred to as North-East Ulster. The population of those four counties alone is about five times as much as the population of Newfoundland, which you have never compelled to go into union with any country. It is as large as the population of New Zealand or larger, I think a great deal larger, and it is very nearly as large, if not as large, as the whole white population of South Africa. In these circumstances, is our demand an extravagant one, that with a population such as that we should be excluded from the operation of a Bill that we loathe? . . . How will Ulster be better under the Bill? In what single respect, what single advantage will Ulster get under the Bill? . . . she will be degraded from her position in this House, and she will be put into a perpetual minority in the House in Dublin, and the great and expanding industries in the North of Ireland will be at the mercy and governed, by whom? . . . some three or four hundred thousand small farmers with the labourers attached, in the South and West of Ireland, with whom they have nothing whatsoever in common, either in ideal or objects, or race or religion, or anything that makes up a homogeneous nation. And what are the material advantages that you hold out to Ulster? Can you tell us one or a fraction of one? It is all the other way. In Belfast, at all events, and in some of the larger towns around it, you are dealing with men who have to engage in great businesses, and you have given us in the Bill the rottenest finance that has ever been proposed in this House . . . . . . there is nothing in the Bill that improves the material condition or can improve the material condition of Ulster . . .

Hansard, 1 January 1913. Ser. 5, Vol. 46: 383–5

D *John Redmond replies.*

... This Home Rule question is for us the demand of a nation for the restoration of its national rights ... In answer to the right hon. Gentleman [Carson], who asks, 'Will you coerce the North-East portion of Ulster to live under a rule they detest?' I ask, will you, if this Bill fails by force, coerce the rest of Ireland to continue to live under a system of rule established at the Union which they loathe and have loathed from that day to this? I say this is a national movement in Ireland. This movement never could have survived the famine, the periods of emigration, the unsuccessful insurrections, and the apparently useless sacrifice of life and of liberty on the scaffold and in the cell, were it not that the soul of the movement was the distinct and indestructible nationality of Ireland.

Ireland for us is one entity. It is one land. Tyrone and Tyrconnell are as much a part of Ireland as Munster or Connaught. Some of the most glorious chapters connected with our national struggle have been associated with Ulster ...

Hansard, 1 January 1913. Ser. 5, Vol. 46: 405–6

Questions

1 In what ways does Carson claim that Ulster would suffer under the Home Rule Bill?
2 On what grounds does Carson claim that Ulster might be separated from the rest of Ireland and Redmond that Ireland should remain united?
3 How accurate was Redmond's claim that 'the principle of devolving on local assemblies the management of local affairs' was 'the foundation of the Empire' in 1912?[1]
4 How far do these sources taken together suggest that Unionists and Nationalists in Ireland were irreconcilable in 1912–13?

Notes

1 See, for example,
Read D 1979 *England 1868–1914* Longman, Chap. 29
Wood A 1982 *Nineteenth Century Britain 1815–1914* Longman, 2nd edn, Chap. 24

9 Late Victorian and Edwardian Society

9.1 The Working Class Standard of Living, 1889–1914

Many of the problems which bedevil any attempt to calculate early nineteenth-century living standards (see section 2.1) arise again at the end of the century, despite the greater availability of data and the pioneering work of the statisticians G H Wood and A L Bowley at the turn of the century. The lines on the graph in Source A thus represent inevitably imperfect estimates, not statistical certainties.

The indexes which Bowley and Wood compiled are based on wage rates, not total earnings, and although Wood made adjustments for unemployment he did so on the basis of trade union figures which are not necessarily representative of the whole workforce. Wood's price index was 'frankly experimental' and Bowley's index, which is normally used, has many imperfections. Goods prices are based partly on retail and partly on wholesale rates, and food prices are taken from London alone. Allowance is made for rent, but on the basis of intermittent figures and again without reflecting the range of regional variations. Bowley himself did not venture to call his table a set of real-wage figures 'because of the numerous qualifications with which it must be used'.

Phelps Brown and Browne's calculations published in 1968 rely on Bowley and Wood's data and therefore incorporate the same imperfections.[1] Other evidence in this section is very different, but, though varied in type, again raises major problems in interpretation.

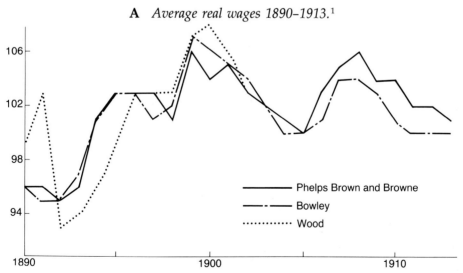

A *Average real wages 1890–1913.*[1]

Phelps Brown and Browne
Bowley
Wood

From: Gourvish T R 'The standard of living.' In: O'Day A (ed) 1979 *The Edwardian Age: Conflict and Stability 1900–1914* Macmillan, p 14

B   *A slum scene, 1889.*

C   *From a book by the Labour politician, Philip Snowden, advocating a legal minimum wage, 1912.*

New expenses have come into the category of necessaries. The development of tramways, the coming of the half penny newspaper, the cheap but better-class music hall and the picture palace, the cheap periodicals and books, the very municipal enterprise which was intended to provide free libraries, free parks, free concerts, has added to the expenditure of the working classes . . .

Snowden P 1912 *The Living Wage*, p 66. In: Read D
1979 *England 1868–1914* Longman, p 403

D   *Rowntree summarises some conclusions from a famous study he made of poverty in York at the end of the nineteenth century. He refers to Charles Booth's study published in 'Life and Labour of the People in London'.*

. . . for a family of father, mother, and three children, the minimum weekly expenditure upon which physical efficiency can be maintained in York is 21s 8d., made up as follows:–

	s.	d.
Food	12	9
Rent (say)	4	0
Clothing, light, fuel, etc.	4	11
	21	8

The necessary expenditure for families larger or smaller than the above will be correspondingly greater or less. This estimate was based upon the assumptions that the diet is selected with a careful regard to the nutritive values of various food stuffs, and that these are all purchased at the lowest current prices. It only allows for a diet less generous as regards variety than that supplied to able-bodied paupers in workhouses. It further assumes that no clothing is purchased which is not absolutely necessary for health, and assumes too that it is of the plainest and most economical description.

No expenditure of any kind is allowed beyond that which is absolutely necessary for the maintenance of *merely physical efficiency*.

The number of persons whose earnings are so low that they cannot meet the expenditure necessary for the above standard of living, stringent to severity though it is, and bare of all creature comforts, was shown to be no less than 7230, or almost exactly 10 per cent of the total population of the city. These persons, then, represent those who are in 'primary' poverty.

... The investigators, in the course of their house-to-house visitation, noted those families who were obviously living in a state of poverty, i.e. in obvious want and squalor ...

In this way 20,302 persons, or 27.84 per cent of the total population, were returned as living in poverty. Subtracting those whose poverty is 'primary', we arrive at the number living in 'secondary' poverty – viz. 13,072, or 17.93 per cent of the total population ...

Mr Booth estimated that 30.7 per cent of the total population of London were living in poverty ... We have been accustomed to look upon the poverty in London as exceptional, but when the result of careful investigation shows that the proportion of poverty in London is practically equalled in what may be regarded as a typical provincial town, we are faced by the startling probability that from 25 to 30 per cent of the town populations of the United Kingdom are living in poverty ...

Rowntree B S 1913 *Poverty, a Study of Town Life*
1913 edn, pp 351–6. In: Read D (ed) 1973
Documents from Edwardian England
Harrap, pp 206–8

Questions

1 What conclusions can be drawn about changes in real wages between 1890 and 1913 from Source A?

2 What indications are there of poverty in Source B and what problems are there in using this as evidence of conditions among poorer members of the working class in London?

3 Consider what problems would be involved in the calculations, estimates and assumptions which Rowntree outlines in Source D.

4 How far do the sources in this section give differing impressions of working class living standards and how would you account for the differences? How would you reconcile the varying evidence here?

Notes

1 Sources for graph:
Wood G H 1909 'Average real wages, allowing for unemployment.' In: 'Real Wages and the Standard of Comfort since 1850.' *J Royal Statistical Society* LXXIII, pp 102–3
Bowley A L 1937 *Wages and Income in the United Kingdom since 1860* Cambridge University Press, p 30
Phelps Brown E H, Browne M 1968 Wage earnings 'in composite units of consumables'. *A Century of Pay*, pp 444–5

9.2 Riches and Poverty – Did Social Divisions Intensify?

Whatever the change in working class living standards, striking contrasts remained between the social and economic condition of different classes. Analysis of income tax returns and Rowntree's social investigations improved public knowledge of these differences, and an increase in conspicuous consumption among the middle and upper classes with the development of luxury hotels, grandiose department stores, yachts and motor cars probably heightened awareness of them. Beyond these contrasts in wealth there were differences in social thinking and perception which cannot be quantified, or perhaps even precisely defined, but which underlay much political and economic debate at the start of the twentieth century.

A   *R Dudley Baxter's estimate of national income in 1867.*

ENGLAND AND WALES, 1867

GROSS INCOME OF ALL CLASSES.

	Persons with Independent Incomes	Amount of Incomes
		£
Upper and Middle Classes . . .	2,053,000	407,200,000
Manual Labour Class	7,785,000	254,729,000
TOTAL	9,838,000	£661,929,000

Baxter R D 1868 *National Income: The United Kingdom* Macmillan, p 52

B   *A description of those in families paying income tax, estimated at about a million.*

. . . Their assured, curt voices, their proud carriage, their clothes, the similarity of their manners, all show that they belong to a caste and that the caste has been successful in the struggle for life. It is called the middle-class, but it ought to be called the upper-class, for nearly everything is below it. I go to the Stores, to Harrod's Stores, to Barker's, to Rumpelmeyer's, to the Royal Academy, and to a dozen clubs in Albemarle Street and Dover Street, and I see again just the same crowd, well-fed, well-dressed, completely free from the cares which beset at least five-sixths of the English race. They have worries; they have taxis because they must not indulge in motor-cars, hansoms because taxis are an extravagance, and omnibuses because they really must economize. But they never look twice at twopence . . .

Bennett A 1909 *Middle Class*. In: *Books and Persons* Chatto and Windus, 1920, p 67. Reprinted in: Read D (ed) 1973 *Documents from Edwardian England* Harrap, p 44

c *An advertisement from 1895.*

HAMPTON & SONS.

TASTEFUL FURNISHING
AT SMALL OUTLAY.

SPECIALISTS IN
THE DECORATIVE
TREATMENT OF
INTERIORS.

MANUFACTURERS
OF ARTISTIC FUR-
NITURE, CAR-
PETS, CURTAINS.

DEALERS IN
WORKS OF ART.

"A glance through this 'Book of Interiors and Furniture' reveals at once the real source of Messrs. Hampton & Sons' success as furnishers, as the contents show that rooms can nowadays be furnished in a quite elegant manner at a comparatively trifling outlay.

"It is by their skill in achieving this end that Hampton & Sons have built up their immense business, and this book of examples evidences that it is upon this ability to put tastefully furnished Homes within the reach of the most modest incomes that the House still relies for its chief support."
Illustrated London News, September 1, 1894.

QUEEN ANNE MORNING ROOM. From the "INTERIORS" in HAMPTON & SONS' CATALOGUE

Wall Panelling	pine, primed for Painting, 2s. per foot super.	Table in solid mahogany, 75s.
Mantel and Overmantel	do. 18 guineas.	Four-fold Screen, do. with tapestry panels, £9 15s.
Overdoor	do. 25s.	Two Easy Chairs, in tapestry, 70s. each. Arm Chair, 55s.
Bookcases	do. 50s. per foot run.	Brass pierced Fender, 45s.
Cabinet in solid mahogany	do. 19 guineas.	Set of Brass Firelrons, 12s. 6d.

SUPPLIED FREE OF CHARGE: Suggestive Sketches and Exact Estimates for Furnishing Single Rooms or Entire Houses.

HAMPTON & SONS' BOOK OF INTERIORS AND FURNITURE SENT FREE TO APPLICANTS WHO CONTEMPLATE FURNISHING. SEPARATELY BOUND DEPARTMENTAL SECTIONS SENT TO THOSE WHO REQUIRE ONLY ONE OR TWO ARTICLES.

HAMPTON & SONS, PALL MALL EAST, LONDON, S.W.

The *Illustrated London News*, 19 January 1895

D   *Sir Leo Chiozza Money's estimate of incomes in 1904.*

BRITISH INCOMES IN 1904

RICH 1,250,000 persons £585,000,000	COMFORTABLE 3,750,000 persons £245,000,000
POOR 38,000,000 PERSONS £880,000,000	

The Aggregate Income of the 43,000,000 people of the United Kingdom is approximately £1,710,000.
1¼ million persons take £585,000,000;
3¾ million persons take £245,000,000;
38 million persons take £880,000,000.

Chiozza Money L G 1905 *Riches and Poverty* frontispiece

E *C F G Masterman comments on the upper and middle class lifestyle, 1909.*

... The whole standard of life has been sensibly raised, not so much in comfort as in ostentation ... Where one house sufficed, now two are demanded; where a dinner of a certain quality, now a dinner of a superior quality; where clothes or dresses or flowers, now more clothes, more dresses, more flowers ...

[The middle class male population] finds itself towards evening in its own territory in the miles and miles of little red houses in little silent streets, in number defying imagination. Each boasts its pleasant drawing room, its bow-window, its little front garden, its high-sounding title – 'Acacia Villa', or 'Camperdown Lodge' – attesting unconquered human aspiration ...

Masterman C F G 1909 *The Condition of England,* Methuen, pp 21–2, 70

F *Rowntree describes how a family with an income at the poverty line would have to spend their money to maintain physical efficiency.*

... A family living upon the scale allowed for in this estimate must never spend a penny on railway fare or omnibus. They must never go into the country unless they walk. They must never purchase a halfpenny newspaper or spend a penny to buy a ticket for a popular concert. They must write no letters to absent children, for they cannot afford to pay the postage. They must never contribute anything to their church or chapel, or give any help to a neighbour which costs them money. They cannot save, nor can they join sick club or Trade Union, because they cannot pay the necessary subscriptions. The children must have no pocket money for dolls, marbles, or sweets. The father must smoke no tobacco, and must drink no beer. The mother must never buy any pretty clothes for herself or for her children ...

Rowntree B S 1913 *Poverty, a Study of Town Life,* 1913 edn, p 167. In: Read D (ed) 1973 *Documents from Edwardian England* Harrap, p 203

Questions

1 Compare the distribution of wealth in 1867 and 1904 as shown in Sources A and D.

2 Compare the economic position of the well-off middle class and poor working class as indicated in Sources B and F. Note from the last section that nearly 10 per cent of York's population had an income below Rowntree's poverty line and nearly 18 per cent were in secondary poverty as they did not spend their incomes with quite the disciplined efficiency he outlines in Source F.

3 Of what value are advertisements like Source C as historical evidence?

4 Money, Masterman and Rowntree were all strong advocates of social change. How far does this affect the value of the evidence in Sources D, E and F?

5 On what grounds may the inequalities and contrasts in wealth shown in these sources be condemned and how might they be defended?

10 The Rise of a Labour Movement

10.1 The Ideas of Socialism

Socialist thinking was not new in late nineteenth-century Britain. Socialist beliefs in greater equality and workers' control over the production of wealth were expressed in the early nineteenth century, and the idea of a labourer's right to the whole product of his labour was influential in the time of the Chartists (see sections 2.2, 3.4). But an important range of socialist publications did become available in the 1880s. What impact might they have had on working men?

A *From 'Progress and Poverty' by the American Henry George, published in London in 1881.*

There is but one way to remove an evil – and that is, to remove its cause. Poverty deepens as wealth increases, and wages are forced down while productive power grows, because land, which is the source of all wealth and the field of all labor, is monopolized. To extirpate poverty, to make wages what justice commands they should be, the full earnings of the laborer, we must therefore substitute for the individual ownership of land a common ownership. Nothing else will go to the cause of evil – in nothing else is there the slightest hope.

George H 1881 *Progress and Poverty* Kegan Paul, p 295

B *From 'The Social Reconstruction of England', 1884, by H M Hyndman, founder of the Social Democratic Federation.*

What we have to-day, I repeat, is a class which owns all the means of production, including the land on the one side. Those who belong to this class escape, as a body, without any sort of manual labor, and live in luxury far in excess of what is beneficial even to them. On the other side is a class utterly destitute of the means of production. Those who belong to this class are, therefore, obliged to compete with one another, in order to gain the scantiest livelihood, and sell their force of labor for miserable wages to the capitalists, who 'exploit' it. Hence increasing wealth and deepening poverty . . .

Hyndman H M 1884 *The Social Reconstruction of England*, p 6. In: Hobsbawm E J (ed) 1948 *Labour's Turning Point* Lawrence and Wishart, p 41

C   *Tables showing average incomes and an*
extract from a section on The Class War in
Sydney Webb's 'Facts for Socialists', first
published by the Fabian Society in 1887.

 £135; average annual product of the
whole community, per adult male.

 £320; average annual income of the
comparatively rich (including non-
workers), per adult male.

 £70; average annual income of the
poor, per adult male.

 £1,665; average annual income, per
adult male, of the gentry, about
222,000 families.

Even if the whole 'manual labor class' made the best possible use of the £35 per adult, which is their average income, it would still be imposs-ible for them to live the cultured human life which the other classes demand for themselves as the minimum of the life worth living. It is practically inevitable that many of the poor, being debarred from this, should endeavor to enjoy themselves in ways not permanently advantageous to themselves or to society.

The force by which this conflict of interests is maintained, without the conscious contrivance of either party, is competition, diverted, like other forces, from its legitimate social use.

Facts for Socialists Fabian Society, 3rd edn, 1890, p 12

D   *From the English translation of Marx and*
Engels' 'Communist Manifesto' published
in 1888.

... Wage-labour rests exclusively on competi-tion between the labourers. The advance of industry, whose involuntary promoter is the bourgeoisie[1], replaces the isolation of the labourers, due to competition, by their revolu-tionary combination, due to association. The development of Modern Industry, therefore,

cuts from under its feet the very foundation on which the bourgeoisie produces and appro-priates products. What the bourgeoisie there-fore produces, above all, are its own grave-diggers. Its fall and the victory of the proletariat[2] are equally inevitable.

... Let the ruling classes tremble at a Commu-nistic revolution. The proletarians have nothing to lose but their chains. They have a world to win.

Working men of all countries unite!

Engels F (ed) 1888 *Authorized English translation of the Manifesto of the Communist Party*, pp 16, 31

Questions

1 What were 'the means of production' (Source B line 2)?
2 What reason do Marx and Engels give in Source D for the development of modern industry cutting from under its feet 'the very foundation on which the bour-geoisie produces and appropriates pro-ducts' (Source D lines 8–9)?
3 What claims in Sources A, B and D might stimulate working men to action?

4 How far could the extract from *Facts for Socialists* in Source C be used to support Hyndman's argument in Source B?

5 With reference to Chapter 9 and your own knowledge assess how far Hyndman was correct in his description of 'deepening poverty' among the late nineteenth-century labour force (Source B line 14).[3]

Notes

1 Bourgeoisie – those who gain wealth from others' labours (for example, industrialists and traders)
2 Proletariat – wage-earning employees
3 See, for example:
Read D 1979 *England 1868–1914* Longman, Chaps. 2, 12

10.2   New Unionism

Small local trade societies which developed in the eighteenth and nineteenth centuries gave way to more national, centrally organised unions in the mid-nineteenth century, but unionism remained largely restricted to an elite of more skilled or highly paid workers. Trade union activity accelerated and broadened during trade booms, and this was particularly marked in 1889–91 when a new, more militant unionism emerged among unskilled workers. The most obvious signs of this 'New Unionism' were a successful London dock strike in 1889 and the growth of general unions which contained a range of labourers from different industries grouped together in one organisation.

Eric Hobsbawm[1] saw these new general unions as 'offspring of a marriage between the class unionism of the socialists and the more modest plans of the unskilled', while Clegg, Fox and Thompson[2] have argued that their form owed more to a realistic calculation of tactical bargaining possibilities. How did the new unions differ from the old and how much were they a product of working class solidarity and socialist influence?

A   *A description of John Burns, one of the dockers' leaders, addressing about 3000 men who met to form a dockers' union at Canning Town before the London strike.*

. . . He winds up with the phrase now historical, and thoroughly his own:- 'No kings, no frontiers, no masters,' and impresses upon all that the first step to this desirable state of things is by reduction of hours of labour, so as to give men time to think and combine.

The Labour Elector, 10 August 1889

B   *From 'The Great Dock Strike' by the socialist H H Champion, published in 1890.*

For many years now the orators of the various sections of Socialists have thundered against the iniquities of the rich at the Dock Gates. Yet in their hour of need the Dockers would accept the aid of three only of the dozens of speakers whose indictments of society in general they must so often have heard. There is no doubt whatever that those Socialists who took part in the strike were welcomed not because of their Socialism, but in spite of it; not on account of their speculative opinions, but for the sake of their personal ability to help . . .

Champion H H 1890 *The Great Dock Strike* Swan Sonnenschein, pp 11–12

C   *Notice in The Workman's Times, 14 November 1890.*

Tyneside and National Labour Union
The monthly report of the above association . . . states . . . On several occasions recently

questions have been asked of statesmen and politicians at public meetings by members of our society who have been described as officials of the Tyneside National Labour Union, your executive desires it to be understood that as a society of workmen this organisation is non-political . . .

The Workman's Times, 14 November 1890

D *The London dockers' leaders Tom Mann and Ben Tillett outline the principles of New Unionism, 1890.*

It is quite true that most of the newly-formed unions pay contributions for trade purposes only, leaving sick and funeral benefits to be dealt with by sick and insurance societies. The work of the trade unionist is primarily to obtain such a re-adjustment of conditions between employers and employed as shall secure to the latter a better share of the wealth they produce, in the form of reduced working hours and higher wages; and our experience has taught us that many of the older unions are very reluctant to engage in a labour struggle, no matter how great the necessity, because they are hemmed in by sick and funeral claims, so that to a large extent they have lost their true characteristic of being fighting organisations, and the sooner they revert to their original programme the better for the well-being of the working masses. We, therefore, advocate strongly the necessity for labour organisations dealing with trade matters only . . .

In conclusion, we repeat that the real difference between the 'new' and the 'old' is, that those who belong to the latter, and delight in being distinct from the policy endorsed by the 'new', do so because they do not recognise, as we do, that it is the work of the trade unionist to stamp out poverty from the land. They do not contend, as we contend, that existing unions should exert themselves to extend organisations where they as yet do not exist . . . Our ideal is a Co-operative Commonwealth . . . The abolition of systematic overtime, material reductions of working hours, elimination of sweaters, an ever-increasing demand for a more righteous share of the wealth created by labour – all these are points in our programme, not one of which can be delayed . . .

Mann T, Tillett B 1890 *The 'New' Trades Unionism: A Reply to Mr George Shipton* Green and McAllan, pp 9, 15

E *George Howell, a former leader of the bricklayers' union and secretary of the TUC Parliamentary Committee, criticises the New Unions and claims that:*

. . . in all essential particulars, the constitution and aims of all bona fide Unions are practically the same; that the difference between one trade society and another consists mainly in the class and kind of 'benefits' provided for, and assured to, members by the rules; and that the real difference, such as it is, which exists between the Old and the New Trade Unionism, is rather to be found in the acknowledged policy, means used, and ulterior objects sought by the new leaders, as formulated in their speeches, contributions to the press, and by resolutions passed at various meetings, than in the constitution and procedure of the Unions themselves.

Howell G 1891 *Trade Unionism New and Old*, p 234

Questions

1 How do Mann and Tillett argue that the New Unionism differs from the old in Source D and in what ways does Howell disagree with them in Source E?
2 What are the main problems in using Sources A–D to assess the strength of socialism in the new unions?
3 What is your overall conclusion about the influence of socialism on dock workers and general unions from these sources? Explain your answer.
4 How far did the unions take up the functions suggested for them in Source D during the years 1888–1900?[3]

Notes

1 Hobsbawm E J 1964 *Labouring Men* Weidenfeld and Nicolson, Chap. 10
2 Clegg H A, Fox A, Thompson A F 1964 *A History of British Trade Unions since 1889*, Vol. 1, Oxford University Press
3 For a shorter trade union history and summaries of historical debate, see:
Lovell J 1977 *British Trade Unions, 1875–1933* Macmillan
Browne H 1979 *The Rise of British Trade Unions, 1825–1914* Longman
Pelling H 1987 *A History of British Trade Unionism* Penguin, 4th edn

10.3 Was the Taff Vale Decision Right or Wrong?

The trade unions' legal position and picketing rights were a matter of prolonged controversy in the late nineteenth century. Picketing was allowed by the 1875 Conspiracy and Protection of Property Act so long as the pickets were only obtaining or communicating information. Nevertheless, at the end of the century it was the subject of a series of legal actions culminating in the Taff Vale case of 1900–1. Workers on the Taff Vale railway in South Wales had gone on strike in August 1900: their employers had arranged an alternative labour force from the National Free Labour Association to break the strike and keep their railway running and the trade unionists had replied with extensive picketing. After the strike the Taff Vale Railway Company sued the men's union, the Amalgamated Society of Railway Servants, for damages, and the House of Lords, the highest court in the land, eventually ruled that the union could be held legally responsible for its members' actions and should pay the company £23 000 for losses during the strike. This created a legal precedent which was in force until 1906 when the decision was reversed

and the legal position altered under the Trade Disputes Act initiated by a Labour MP. Was the Taff Vale decision right or wrong?

A *'The Railway Review', the weekly paper of the Amalgamated Society of Railway Servants, comments on the position just after the Taff Vale strike.*

The present state of the law, or, at any rate, its interpretation by learned judges, is a monstrous injustice to working men. It is obviously one-sided and unfair. A Trade Unionist may not persuade – he can only communicate information; he may not distribute a handbill telling a man he will be a blackleg if he takes up work in a strike – that is a libel. But an employer may hire a gang of ruffians who will capture all the riff-raff they can get hold of, this gang may lock men in waiting rooms and railway carriages, may forcibly escort them along streets and works guarded by police, may confine them in rooms on the premises, and watch over them while they do other people's work. This is the fairness of the law. This is how men are *persuaded* to work. This is *free* labour . . .

The Railway Review, 7 September 1900

B *The employers' paper 'The Railway News' comments on the situation.*

The principal lessons of the strike are few, but they are valuable: First, that there is no difficulty in obtaining as many new hands as are wanted; and, second, that protection is the sole difficulty to be surmounted . . . The crowning victory of the company was, however, the success of the application for an injunction against the leaders of the strike, which was dead from that success. No strike can succeed except by intimidation, which is the striker's only weapon; with picketing impossible, there can be no effective intimidation . . . this power has been maintained by the peculiar position of the unions, which have hitherto been regarded as outside the jurisdiction of the courts . . .

The Railway News, 8 September 1900

C *William Collison of the National Free Labour Association describes the arrival of his men at Cardiff station.*

... the station was filled with Union pickets, and twenty-eight of my men were forcibly made prisoners, marched to the Union headquarters in Cathays, locked in, and then when the time arrived, marched back to the station and entrained for London ...

Collison W 1913 *The Apostle of Free Labour,* pp 141–2
In: Hobsbawm E J (ed) 1948 *Labour's Turning Point*
Lawrence and Wishart

D *Richard Bell, General Secretary of the Amalgamated Society of Railway Servants, discusses the strike and the decision made by the House of Lords in 1901.*

[The strike] was organised and brought about without consultation with or sanction from the Executive Committee or responsible officials. But immediately after the men decided to strike they appealed to the Executive Committee for support. After considerable discussion and a division of opinion, the Executive Committee, by a majority of one, granted the request ... The strike lasted a fortnight. During the progress of the dispute certain unlawful acts in picketing were alleged to have taken place, and upon these allegations the Company applied for an injunction against the A.S.R.S. ...

In reviewing the strikes that have taken place during recent years – say, the last five years – it will be found that the greatest number of them have been unauthorised by the respective Unions. They have generally been commenced by some section of the members, and the Executives afterwards appealed to for support, which invariably has been given.

This may rightly be termed as abusing the privilege enjoyed ... Strikes, started in many instances without sufficient consideration as to cause, and too often none as to the chances of success or consequences. A very large percentage of these strikes have been unsuccessful. The men gaining nothing, but losing a great deal, besides losses to employers and inconvenience

to the public. The latter at any rate, being an item which cannot be ignored in these days.

... The Unions, by this judge-made law, can now be made liable for damages caused by the action of their Executives or officials. Those who will feel the result most will be the industrial Jingoes, for we have, unfortunately, some who are as eager for strikes as others are for war ...

The members of the various Unions will have to see that they elect their strongest men on the Executives and the most level-headed men as their officials. The Executives must, in turn, insist upon the rules of the Societies being strictly adhered to ...

The Clarion, 3 August 1901

E *Walter Hudson, a Labour MP from the Amalgamated Society of Railway Servants, moves the second Reading of his Trade Unions and Trade Disputes Bill which provided the basis for a new law in 1906.*

... The Taff Vale judgment was a creation of new law, inasmuch as it never previously existed in either statute law or decision of any Court ... if injury to trade unions was not desired, or desirable, on the part of the employers, what was the good of having the power to sue? It was not only the clear intention of the framers of the Act, but the Act of 1871 actually did leave to trade unions the immunity which for thirty years they had enjoyed. They did not want any specially created privilege, but merely asked to be restored to the original position of immunity. They asked for an equality before the law ... The fallacy of the conclusion that collective responsibility on the part of unions was, or could be, an effective means and incentive to more cautious action was entirely without foundation. Who had suffered most during the past five years of abundance of trade union litigation? Not the officials and leaders as a rule, but the rank and file of the members, many of whom knew nothing of the actual merits of the action brought against [them] in their collective capacity ...

Hansard, 30 March 1906. Ser. 4, Vol. 155: 26

Questions

1 In what contrasting ways do *The Railway Review* and *The Railway News* claim that the legal position has been unfair up to the autumn of 1900?
2 How could Collison's description in Source C be used to:
   a Support the argument in Source B?
   b Show workers' solidarity behind the strike?
3 How does Bell suggest that the Taff Vale decision might be in the best interests of ordinary trade union members in Source D and how does Hudson argue that this was not the case in Source E?
4 How would you attempt to assess which of the two is more representative of trade union opinion?
5 Do you think the Taff Vale decision was right or wrong? Justify your answer.

10.4   The Early Labour Party – Socialist Spearhead or Liberal Fringe Group?

In 1900 a number of trade unions and socialist societies joined to found the Labour Representation Committee (LRC) which worked to get Labour candidates into Parliament. The 29 LRC MPs returned at the 1906 General Election then formed the Parliamentary Labour Party. In retrospect this appears to be very important as the start of the twentieth-century Labour party, but how far was it a socialist group or just the left-wing fringe of the Liberal party?

A   *Extracts from a debate at the 1907 Labour party conference.*

W. ATKINSON (Paper Stainers) moved the following substitution for Clause II of the Constitution:

1 This annual conference of the Labour Party hereby declares that its ultimate object shall be the obtaining for the workers the full results of their labour by the overthrow of the present competitive system of capitalism, and the institution of a system of public ownership and control of all the means of life.
2 To organize and maintain a Parliamentary Labour Party with its own whips and whose policy shall be in the direction of attaining the above, and also of carrying out the decisions of the annual conferences.

He said the Labour Party ought to have an object worthy of attainment. They recognized that there was something more desirable than merely obtaining a number of representatives inside the House of Commons. A number of years ago even to discuss such an object would have been considered idealistic, but anything less than this as an ideal was now looked upon by ordinary working men as insufficient and incomplete ...

PETE CURRAN (Gas Workers) said that as a Socialist he opposed this amendment of the constitution. The Socialist section was bound in honour to acknowledge that the delegates had not yet declared in favour of class-conscious principles ... Surely the mover and seconder realized that the carrying of this resolution would be the destruction of the Movement as it existed today. If they did not, they did not understand the Movement as he understood it. The Trade Unionists, who made up the bulk of the Movement, and contributed the funds of the Movement, would not pledge themselves to this class-consciousness. They had got them out of the old rut of political neutrality into the position of political independence, and the promoters of that amendment wanted to clear them out of the Movement. That would not be in the interests of the solidarity of the Movement, and he would resent with all his vigour this kind of back-handed attempt to create dissension.

... A card vote showed 98,000 in favour of the amendment, and 835,000 against.

Labour Party Annual Conference Report.
In: Beattie A (ed) 1970 *English Party Politics*
Vol. II, Weidenfeld and Nicolson,
pp 258–62

B   *The first page of a Labour party leaflet, published for the January 1910 General Election.*

Labour Party Leaflet, No. 38.   250th Thousand.

WHY YOU SHOULD
VOTE FOR THE
LABOUR CANDIDATES
BECAUSE

1.—The shameful neglect of Social and Economic questions by Conservative and Liberal Governments in the past rendered it absolutely necessary for the Workers to be directly represented in Parliament by men who would press with persistence for the practical handling of such questions by parliament.

Necessitous School Children are fed; a Minimum Wage has been established in Sweated Industries; six hundred thousand Aged People now receive Old Age Pensions.

2.—The vast army of Unemployed men and women provide striking proof that Unemployment is now inseparable from competitive industry, and it is, therefore, rather permanent than temporary in character. It is one of our gravest and most painful social evils and causes an unparalleled amount of privation, suffering, and despair.

The Labour Party is the only political Party that recognises and supports the **Right-to-Work** and the **Right-to-Live**.

3.—The Labour Members are practical men, having served in the mine, the factory, and the workshop. As a result of their experience they helped to strengthen and extend the Workman's Compensation Act, so that when it became law its benefits applied to nearly three millions of workers omitted when the Bill was introduced.

The cost of Labour Representation is more than returned by the greater amount of Compensation to which the wage-earners are now entitled.

4.—The Labour Party are convinced that thousands of fatal and non-fatal accidents in mines, quarries, factories and workshops are preventible, as they are in many cases the outcome of the system under which the workers are employed.

They have urged for enquiries into the causes of accidents, and for the appointment of additional numbers of Mining and Factory Inspectors with practical experience.

Labour Party Leaflet, No. 38

C   *Ramsay MacDonald, the Chairman of the Labour party from 1911 to 1914 explains the party's position.*

The Labour Party is not Socialist. It is a union of Socialist and trade-union bodies for immediate political work ... But it is the only political form which evolutionary Socialism can take in a country with the political traditions and methods of Great Britain. Under British conditions, a Socialist Party is the last, not the first, form of the Socialist movement in politics.

Ramsay MacDonald J 1911 *The Socialist Movement*
Home University Library, p 235

Questions

1 What do you understand by:
   a 'Sweated industries' (Source B section 1, lines 6–7)?
   b The 'Right-to-Work' (Source B section 2, line 6)?

2 In what ways was Atkinson's resolution (Source A) socialist?
3 How extensive were the social and economic changes the leaflet (Source B) advocated and how far was it socialist?
4 What reasons do Sources A and C suggest for the Labour party being slow in progressing towards socialism? What other factors made it difficult for the party to put forward socialist policies?[1]
5 How far were the improvements mentioned in Source B the result of Labour party action?[1]

Notes

1 For questions 4 and 5, see text and topic books, particularly:
Adelman P 1986 *The Rise of the Labour Party 1880–1945* Longman, 2nd edn
Laybourn K 1988 *The Rise of Labour* Edward Arnold

11 Liberal Government 1905–14

11.1 What was the New Liberalism?

The most influential economists and philosophers of the late eighteenth and early nineteenth centuries had generally emphasised economic freedom and the evils of state intervention. But later in the nineteenth century political thinkers were more aware of the need for government action and the limited value of a freedom which just meant absence of outside restrictions. One of the most important was T H Green, an Oxford philosopher and Liberal supporter, who expounded the idea of positive freedom.

Although Gladstone's ministries initiated considerable social change and regulation, Gladstonian Liberalism emphasised independence for the working man rather than any need for state support and social reconstruction. Subsequently, and partly through the influence of Green's philosophy, a 'New Liberalism' developed in the early twentieth century. It emerged through the columns of journals like *The Speaker* and *The Nation*, through the writings of Liberal politicians like C F G Masterman and through the work of David Lloyd George and Winston Churchill who became Chancellor of the Exchequer and President of the Board of Trade in the Liberal government Asquith formed in 1908. What was the 'New Liberalism' and why did it develop?

A *T H Green explains positive freedom.*

We shall probably all agree that freedom, rightly understood, is the greatest of blessings – that its attainment is the true end of all our effort as citizens. But when we thus speak of freedom, we should consider carefully what we mean by it. We do not mean merely freedom from restraint or compulsion. We do not mean merely freedom to do as we like irrespective of what it is that we like. We do not mean a freedom that can be enjoyed by one man or one set of men at the cost of a loss of freedom to others. When we speak of freedom as something to be so highly prized, we mean a positive power or capacity of doing or enjoying something worth doing or enjoying, and that, too, something that we do or enjoy in common with others. We mean by it a power which each man exercises through the help or security given him by his fellow-men, and which he in turn helps to secure for them. When we measure the progress of a society by its growth in freedom, we measure it by the increasing development and exercise on the whole of those powers of contributing to social good with which we believe the members of the society to be endowed – in short, by the greater power on the part of the citizens as a body to make the most and best of themselves.

Green T H 1881 *Liberal Legislation and Freedom of Contract*, pp 9–10. In: Bullock A, Shock M (eds) 1967 *The Liberal Tradition from Fox to Keynes* Oxford University Press, p 180

B *From Lloyd George speaking to a meeting in November 1904.*

We have a great Labour Party sprung up. Unless we can prove, as I think we can, that there is no necessity for a separate party in order to press forward the legitimate claims of labour, then you will find that the same thing will happen in England that has happened in Belgium and Germany – that the Liberal Party will be practically wiped out, and that in its place you will get a more extreme and revolutionary party, which will sail under the colours of Socialism or Independent Labour.

I don't think that will be necessary. I think it would be a disaster to progress. I think it is better that you should have a Party which combines every section and shade of progressive opinion, taken from all classes of the community, rather than a party which represents one shade of opinion alone and one class of the community alone. – (Hear, hear.) Progress will suffer, I am sure, by a policy of that kind, and it rests with the Liberal Administration which we can see on the horizon to prevent such a state of things from coming about.

Manchester Guardian, 7 November 1904. In: Wrigley C 1976 *David Lloyd George and the British Labour Movement* Harvester Press, p 26

C *From a letter that Churchill wrote to 'The Nation', March 1908.*

Science, physical and political alike, revolts at the disorganisation which glares at us in so many aspects of modern life. We see the curse of unregulated casual employment steadily rotting the under side of the labour market. We see the riddles of unemployment and under-employment quite unsolved. There are mighty trades which openly assert the necessity of a labour surplus – 'on hand' in the streets and round the dock gates – for the ordinary commercial convenience of their business. And they practise what they preach . . . There are other industries which prey upon the future. Swarms of youths, snatched from school at the period in life when training should be most careful and discipline most exacting, are flung into a precocious manhood, and squander their most precious years in erratic occupations, which not only afford no career for them in after life, but sap and demoralise that character without which no career can be discovered or pursued. Thousands of children grow up not nourished sufficiently

to make them effective citizens, or even to derive benefit from the existing educational arrangements . . .

It is false and base to say that these evils, and others like them, too many here to set forth, are inherent in the nature of things, that their remedy is beyond the wit of man, that experiment is foolhardy, that all is for the best in 'Merrie England.' No one will believe it any more.

The Nation, 7 March 1908. In: Morgan K O 1971 *The Age of Lloyd George* Allen and Unwin, pp 146-7

D *C F G Masterman's comment on urban working class life.*

. . . Under darkened skies, and in an existence starved of beauty . . . communities of men and women and children continue their unchanging toil. Is the price being paid too great for the result attained? The cities have sucked in the healthy, stored-up energies of rural England; with an overwhelming percentage today of country upbringing. Must they ever thus be parasitic on another life outside, and this nation divide into breeding grounds for the creation of human energies and consuming centres where these energies are destroyed? . . . . . . No one can pretend that a condition of stable equilibrium exists, in which as to-day, with the removal of supernatural sanctions and promises of future redress, the working people find a political freedom accompanying an economic servitude . . .

Masterman C F G 1909 *The Condition of England* Methuen, pp 109, 155

Questions

1 What do you think Masterman meant by:
  a 'the removal of supernatural sanctions' (Source D lines 14–15)?
  b 'political freedom accompanying an economic servitude' (Source D lines 17–18)?
2 What did T H Green mean by positive freedom (Source A)?

3 In what ways does Churchill show that positive freedom was lacking in Source C?

4 How far do Sources B–D suggest that New Liberalism developed from moral and humanitarian concern, economic needs or political and electoral necessity?

5 Which Liberal reforms were produced in response to the needs and problems outlined in Source C and how far did they go in tackling these problems?[1]

Notes

1 See text and topic books, for example,
Read D 1979 *England 1868–1914* Longman, Chap. 28
Feuchtwanger E J 1985 *Democracy and Empire* Edward Arnold, Chap. 8
Royle E 1987 *Modern Britain, a Social History 1750–1985* Edward Arnold, Chap. 4
May T 1987 *An Economic and Social History of Britain 1760–1970* Longman, Chap. 11
Birch R C 1974 *The Shaping of the Welfare State* Longman, Chap. 3
For further coverage see, for example:
Read D 1972 *Edwardian England 1901–15* Harrap, Chap. 6
Fraser D 1984 *The Evolution of the British Welfare State* Macmillan, 2nd edn, Chap. 7

11.2 The 1909 Budget – A People's Budget or Class Warfare?

One feature of the New Liberalism was a need to raise more money from the rich to finance more welfare provision for the poor. Consequently Lloyd George's 1909 budget brought tax increases, notably higher income tax for the wealthy and a survey to prepare the way for a new land tax. Many of the better off were outraged, and the budget raised fundamental social and constitutional issues.

A *Lloyd George's case for increased taxation in his budget speech.*

. . . unfortunately, I have to reckon not merely with an enormous increase in expenditure this year, but an inevitable expansion of some of the heaviest items in the course of the coming years. To what is the increase in expenditure due? It is very well known that it must be placed to the credit of two items and practically two items alone. One is the Navy and the other is Old Age Pensions . . . The increased expenditure under both heads was substantially incurred with the unanimous assent of all political parties in this House . . .

. . . We are told that we ought not to have touched old age pensions – at least, not at the present moment, when heavy liabilities were in sight in connection with the defence of the country . . . But . . . we had no honourable alternative left. We simply honoured a cheque drawn years ago in favour of the aged poor, which bore at its foot the signature of all the leaders of political parties in this country . . .

. . . next year the Treasury will have to find money for paying the whole cost of construction of four 'Dreadnoughts' during an unbroken period of 12 months. This, in addition to an eleven months' building on the two 'Dreadnoughts' which were laid down some time ago, will bring up the Estimates of the year for Naval construction to a figure which is considerably above even the increased estimate of this year . . .

Now I come to the consideration of the social problems which are urgently pressing for solution – problems affecting the lives of the people. The solution of all these questions involves finance . . . If we put off dealing with these social sores, are the evils which arise from them not likely to grow and to fester, until finally the loss which the country sustains will be infinitely greater than anything it would have to bear in paying the cost of an immediate remedy? . . .

. . . This . . . is a War Budget. It is for raising money to wage implacable warfare against poverty and squalidness . . .

Hansard, 29 April 1909. Ser. 5, Vol. 4: 474–548

B   *The Leader of the Opposition, A J Balfour denounces the Budget at the Annual Demonstration of the Conservative Primrose League in the Royal Albert Hall.*

. . . The Chancellor of the Exchequer told us the other day that [the growth of expenditure] fell mainly under two heads – old age pensions and naval expenditure. Well, so it does in the main. What have we got to say about these two forms of expenditure? On the first I have to say what my friends and I have said consistently for many months past – namely, that while some form of – I will not say old age pensions merely, but some form of insurance against the inevitable accidents of life, be they old age or be they sickness, was of the first importance to the community, the subject itself was so difficult . . . it ought to have been taken in hand with every caution . . . with all the ardour of electioneers they rushed into the first hand-to-mouth scheme which they could find . . . And while they were putting on expenditure they were taking off taxes. (Hear, hear.) While they were priding themselves on giving the great masses of our fellow countrymen some new boon in the way of expenditure they were at the same time removing mainly from those very classes themselves some of the expenditure which might well have been used to achieve these great objects . . .

. . . how about the Navy? . . . The late Government thought – and who looking back, will say they thought wrongly? – that, on the whole, a programme of four Dreadnoughts a year at that time was enough, and not more than enough, to meet the needs of the country. No continuity is pursued by . . . the Government . . . They dropped their construction . . .

The Government . . . have set to work too late in the day, or very late in the day, to urge the contractors to increase their plant and to try and make up the arrears in shipbuilding which ought never to have existed (Cheers) . . .

The Times, 8 May 1909

C   *Lloyd George defends his proposal to tax landowners in a speech at Limehouse in east London.*

Now, all we say is this: 'In future you must pay one halfpenny in the pound on the real value of your land. In addition to that, if the value goes up, not owing to your efforts – if you spend money on improving it we will give you credit for it – but if it goes up owing to the industry and the energy of the people living in that locality, one-fifth of that increment shall in future be taken as a toll by the State.' . . .

What is the landlord's increment? Who is the landlord? The landlord is a gentleman – I have not a word to say about him in his personal capacity – the landlord is a gentleman who does not earn his wealth. He does not even take the trouble to receive his wealth. He has a host of agents and clerks to receive it for him. He does not even take the trouble to spend his wealth. He has a host of people around him to do the actual spending for him. He never sees it until he comes to enjoy it. His sole function, his chief pride is stately consumption of wealth produced by others.

Better Times, Speeches by the Right Hon. D Lloyd George MP 1910, Hodder and Stoughton pp 150–1

D *A cartoon from 'Punch', 28 April 1909.*

RICH FARE.

The Giant Lloyd-Gorgibuster : "FEE, FI, FO, FAT,
I SMELL THE BLOOD OF A PLUTOCRAT;
BE HE ALIVE OR BE HE DEAD,
I'LL GRIND HIS BONES TO MAKE MY BREAD."

Questions

1 What were
  a 'Dreadnoughts' (Source A line 24)?
  b plutocrats (Source D)?
2 How does Lloyd George argue that the tax increases were necessary to finance broadly agreed expenditure in Source A and on what grounds does Balfour deny this in Source B?
3 What alternative, less costly way of financing old age pensions could have been used if they had 'been taken in hand with every caution' (Source B lines 14–15)?
4 Lloyd George was accused of stirring up class warfare.
  a In what ways does Source D suggest this?
  b How far does Source C substantiate the accusation?
5 What other evidence can you find of Lloyd George's involvement in class-based politics in the years 1909–14 and how far do you think the social circumstances of the time justified his position?[1]

Notes

1 See text and topic books and biographies, for example,
  Morgan K O 1974 *Lloyd George* Weidenfeld and Nicolson
  Pugh M 1988 *Lloyd George* Longman
  The major biography of Lloyd George is by John Grigg. See:
  Volume 2 (1978) *Lloyd George: The People's Champion 1902–11*; Volume 3 (1985) *Lloyd George: From Peace to War 1912–1916* Methuen

11.3 The Peers and the Budget

The House of Lords rejected the 'people's budget' by 350 votes to 75. Were they justified?

A *Walter Bagehot described the Lords' role in a nineteenth-century book on the constitution which has been used for reference ever since.*

Since the Reform Act the House of Lords has become a revising and suspending House. It can alter Bills; it can reject Bills on which the House of Commons is not yet thoroughly in earnest – upon which the nation is not yet determined. Their veto is a sort of hypothetical veto. They say, We reject your Bill for this once, or these twice, or even these thrice; but if you keep on sending it up, at last we won't reject it . . .

Bagehot W 1867 *The English Constitution* Chapman and Hall, p 130

B *From a private letter from Balfour to Lord Lansdowne, the Conservative leader in the House of Lords, following their party's defeat in the 1906 General Election.*

The real point is . . . to secure that the Party in the two Houses shall not work as separate armies, but shall co-operate in a common plan of campaign . . . I do not think the House of Lords will be able to escape the duty of making serious modifications in important Government measures . . . I incline to advise that we should fight all points of importance very stiffly in the Commons, and should make the House of Lords the theatre of compromise . . .

British Museum *Balfour Manuscripts* 49729, f 228–30

C *Balfour gives a public view on the role of the House of Lords when speaking in Manchester during the controversy over the budget.*

The object of a second Chamber is not, and never has been, to prevent the people, the mass of the community, the electorate, the constituencies determining what policy they should pursue; it exists for the purpose of seeing that on great issues the policy which is pursued is not the policy of a temporary majority elected for a different purpose, but represents the sovereign convictions of the people that returned the House of Commons for the few years in which it carries their mandate ... its mission and great function is to see that the Government of this country is a popular Government. What it has to do on these fortunately rare, but all the more important, occasions is not to insist that this or that Ministry powerful for the time, once powerful perhaps, no longer powerful it may be, is to be clothed with all the tyrannical powers which we have done so much to prevent anybody in the State, any element in the State, exercising. The object is to see that there shall be referred to the people that which concerns the people, and that the people shall not be betrayed by hasty legislation, interested legislation, legislation having, it may be, some electoral object in view, or some vindictive policy to carry out.

The Times, 18 November 1909. In: Read D (ed) 1972 *Documents from Edwardian England, 1901–15* Harrap, p 260

D *Lord Lansdowne argues that the Peers should reject the 1909 Budget.*

... [a] practice has grown up – quite a recent practice – I mean the practice of grouping together under one Bill a large number of measures dealing with different taxes ... You will observe that the mere fact that this practice was resorted to in itself implies the admission that your Lordships have a right of rejection, because the idea of this practice of 'tacking' Bills was that you could make it more difficult for the Lords to reject a Bill which they desired to reject by tacking it on to another Bill which they did not desire to reject ...

Hansard, 22 November 1909. Ser. 5, Vol. 4: 733

E *Asquith speaks about the constitutional crisis at a great Liberal meeting in the Royal Albert Hall.*

... The immediate, the acutely provoking cause of what is rightly called a constitutional crisis is the entirely new claim put forward by the House of Lords, not only to meddle with, but in effect to control and to mould our national finance. Only once within living memory has the Upper House attempted to touch a single tax imposed or repealed by the House of Commons[1]. That attempt recoiled at once upon their heads, and the claim has never since been renewed ...... Our present condition gives us all the drawbacks, with few, if any, of the advantages of a Second Chamber. For what is our actual Second Chamber? (Laughter). It is a body which has no pretensions or qualifications to be the organ or the interpreter of the popular will. (Cheers). It is a body in which one party in the State is in possession of a permanent and an overwhelming majority. It is a body which, as experience shows, in temper and in action, is frankly and nakedly partisan. It is a body which does not attempt to exercise any kind of effective control over the legislation of the other House when its own party is in a majority there. It is a body which, when the conditions are reversed, however clear and emphatic the verdict of the country may have been, sets itself to work to mutilate and to obstruct democratic legislation, and, even in these last days, to usurp the control of the democratic finance.

... The absolute veto which it at present possesses must go. (Loud and continued cheers). The power which it claims from time to time of, in effect, compelling us to choose between a dissolution and – so far as legislative projects are concerned – legislative sterility – that power must go also.

The people in future when they elect a new House of Commons must be able to feel what they cannot feel now, that they are sending to Westminster men who will have the power, not merely of proposing and debating, but of making laws. (Cheers).

The Daily Chronicle, 11 December 1909

Questions

1 Compare the arguments in Sources C and E over how the Lords' use of its powers helped or hindered the development of democratic government.

2 On what grounds does Asquith claim that the Lords was constitutionally wrong in rejecting the budget and Lansdowne that it was justified in Sources D and E?

3 How far is Balfour's argument in Source C in agreement with Bagehot's statement of the constitution in Source A?

4 **a** How far does Source B from Balfour's private letter support Asquith's claim that the Lords was 'frankly and nakedly partisan' (Source E line 21)?

　b How far did the Lords' actions over the previous 20 years support Asquith's belief?[2]

5 To what extent was the House of Commons democratically elected in 1909?[3]

6 Do you think the House of Lords was justified in rejecting the budget?

Notes

1 The rejection of Gladstone's proposal to remove paper duties, 1860

2 See textbooks

3 See, for example:
Wright D G 1970 *Democracy and Reform 1815–1885* Longman, Part 3
Pugh M 1988 *The Evolution of the British Electoral System 1832–1987* Historical Association
For further discussion of the early twentieth-century franchise, see:
Arnstein W L 1979 'Edwardian politics: Turbulent spring or Indian summer.' In: O'Day A (ed) 1979 *The Edwardian Age: Conflict and Stability 1900–1914* Macmillan; Pugh M 1982 *The Making of Modern British Politics 1867–1939* Blackwell, Chap. 7; Clarke P 1982 'The Edwardians and the constitution.' In: Read D (ed) *Edwardian England* Croom Helm

11.4 The Strange Death of Liberal England and the Rampant Omnibus

The Liberals had won an overwhelming victory at the 1906 General Election, but it was the last time they gained an overall majority in the House of Commons. After World War I they declined rapidly and were replaced by Labour as the main party of the left. How far had the decline set in by 1914?

In 1935 George Dangerfield argued that the Liberals' fall was inevitable as far back as 1906:

... the Liberal Party which came back to Westminster with an overwhelming majority [in 1906] was already doomed. It was like an army protected at all points except for one vital position on its flank. With the election of fifty-three Labour representatives, the death of Liberalism was pronounced; it was no longer the Left ...

Dangerfield G 1935 *The Strange Death of Liberal England* Paladin edn, 1966, p 24

Thirty years later Trevor Wilson produced an opposing argument:

The Liberal Party can be compared to an individual who, after a period of robust health and great exertion, experienced symptoms of illness (Ireland, Labour unrest, the suffragettes). Before a thorough diagnosis could be made, he was involved in an encounter with a rampant omnibus (the First World War), which mounted the pavement and ran him over. After lingering painfully, he expired ...

Wilson T 1966 *The Downfall of the Liberal Party 1914–1935* Collins, p 18

What do General Election results and contemporary political comments suggest about the Liberals' position before World War I?[1]

A *General Election results 1900–10.*

	Total Votes	M.P.s Elected	Candi-dates	Unopposed Returns	% Share of Total Vote	Average % Vote per Opposed Candidate
1900. 28 Sep–24 Oct						
Conservative	1,797,444	402	579	163	51.1	52.5
Liberal	1,568,141	184	406	22	44.6	48.2
Labour	63,304	2	15	..	1.8	26.6
Irish Nationalist	90,076	82	100	58	2.5	80.0
Others	544	..	2	..	.0	2.2
Elec. 6,730,935	3,519,509	670	1,102	243	100.0	..
Turnout 74.6%						
1906. 12 Jan–7 Feb						
Conservative	2,451,454	157	574	13	43.6	44.1
Liberal	2,757,883	400	539	27	49.0	52.6
Labour	329,748	30	51	..	5.9	39.9
Irish Nationalist	35,031	83	87	74	0.6	63.1
Others	52,387	..	22	..	0.9	18.8
Elec. 7,264,608	5,626,503	670	1,273	114	100.0	..
Turnout 82.6%						
1910. 14 Jan–9 Feb						
Conservative	3,127,887	273	600	19	46.9	47.5
Liberal	2,880,581	275	516	1	43.2	49.2
Labour	511,392	40	81	..	7.7	38.4
Irish Nationalist	124,586	82	104	55	1.9	77.7
Others	22,958	..	14	..	0.3	15.4
Elec. 7,694,741	6,667,404	670	1,315	75	100.0	..
Turnout 86.6%						
1910. 2–19 Dec						
Conservative	2,424,566	272	550	72	46.3	47.9
Liberal	2,293,686	272	467	35	43.8	49.5
Labour	376,581	42	59	3	7.2	42.8
Irish Nationalist	131,721	84	106	53	2.5	81.9
Others	8,768	..	9	..	0.2	9.1
Elec. 7,709,981	5,235,322	670	1,191	163	100.0	..
Turnout 81.1%						

Butler D, Freeman J (ed) 1963 *British Political Facts 1900–1960* Macmillan, p 122

B *A writer in the Labour newspaper 'The Clarion' comments on the January 1910 General Election result.*

The Labour Party will go back to Parliament weaker in number by half a dozen, and immeasurably weaker in prestige, than they were in 1906.

What is the reason of this slump in the progress of Labour? Can any-one doubt that the set-back is due to the alliance policy? . . .

The Clarion, 28 January 1910

C *From an article on 'The Elections and their Moral' in the Conservative 'Blackwood's Magazine', March 1910.*

. . . Lancashire and Yorkshire on the whole have given a class vote. The men who applauded a Conservative speaker and heckled a Liberal, when it came to the election day voted not for a principle but for what they had come to regard as their class. The trade union has become not merely an economic but a political organisation. The workman is beginning to stick by his class in politics as for some years he has stuck by it in industrial disputes. The Tory working-man, who used to be common in Lancashire, is fast disappearing. Soon the Liberal working-man will follow suit, and, if we are not alive to the danger, the masses will become one vast automatic machine for registering the decrees of a Labour caucus . . .

Blackwood's Magazine, March 1910. Vol. 187, p 436

D *From the diary of Beatrice Webb, a Labour supporter and member of the Fabian Society, 30 November 1910.*

The big thing that has happened in the last two years is that Lloyd George and Winston Churchill have practically taken the *limelight,* not merely from their own colleagues, but from the Labour Party. They stand out as the most advanced politicians. And, if we get a Liberal majority and payment of members, we shall

have any number of young Fabians rushing for Parliament, fully equipped for the fray – better than the Labour men – and enrolling themselves behind these two radical leaders.

In: Webb B 1948 *Our Partnership* Longman, pp 465–6

E *From a private letter written in June 1914 by C P Scott, editor of 'The Manchester Guardian', a left-wing Liberal paper.*

. . . I confess I am beginning to feel . . . that the existing Liberal party is played out and that if it is to count for anything in the future it must be reconstructed largely on a labour basis.

In: Wilson T (ed) 1970 *The Political Diaries of C. P. Scott 1911–28* Collins, p 88

F *Christopher Addison, a Liberal minister who later joined the Labour Party, records his feelings on the outbreak of World War I.*

Most of us felt that Liberalism was already in its grave – at any rate that is what I feel like.

When one thinks of all our schemes of social reform just set agoing and of those for which plans had been made in this year's Budget, one could weep. Nearly all the things that we have been toiling at for years have come toppling down about our ears. Insurance must go on: the feeding of children is safe: and we must snatch what we can of others. But it is obvious that the war will mop up all the money that has been made available.

Addison C *Four and a Half Years: A Personal Diary,* Vol I, Hutchinson, p 35

Questions

1 **a** What was 'the alliance policy' (Source B line 7)?
  b What do you understand by a 'caucus' (Source C line 16)?
  c Who were the 'Fabians' (Source D line 8)?

2 How far does the table (Source A) suggest that the Liberals were being threatened and undermined by Labour in 1906–14? What factors apart from popular support determined the number of Labour candidates and the vote they received at elections?

3 Which of Sources B–F support Dangerfield's argument and which support Wilson's: how might they be used to do this? Could any of the sources be used to support both arguments and if so how?

4 Sources B–F are all apparently written by people involved in politics and all give interpretations of events which seem contrary to the writers' preferences. How might this affect our evaluation of them as historical evidence?

5 Sources B and C were written for journals which would be read mainly by party supporters while being available to the general public. Sources D, E and F were written in private letters or diaries. How do these factors affect their usefulness to the historian?

6 Sources B–D were written in 1910. Which developments since then might have convinced C P Scott that the Liberal party was 'played out' when he wrote Source E in June 1914? Consider the Liberal government's reforming record, what problems it faced in these years and how well it was able to deal with them.[2]

Notes

1 For a summary of the debate on the Liberal decline, see:
Adelman P 1981 *The Decline of the Liberal Party 1910–1931* Longman, Part 3
Layburn K 1988 *The Rise of Labour* Edward Arnold, Chap. 2

2 See text and topic books, for example:
Feuchtwanger E J 1985 *Democracy and Empire* Edward Arnold, Chap. 8
Aikin K W W 1972 *The Last Years of Liberal England 1900–1914* Collins, Chap. 6
Adelman P 1981 *The Decline of the Liberal Party 1910–1931* Longman, Chap. 1

12 Foreign Policy 1895–1914

12.1 Why Did Britain Fight the Boer War of 1899–1902?

From the time Britain gained Cape Colony on the south-western tip of Africa in 1814 she had a bad relationship with the Boers, who were descendants of Dutch settlers in the area. In the 1830s the Boers escaped from their British rulers by making the Great Trek and founded new colonies which subsequently became the Orange Free State and the Transvaal, but the British would not let them go so easily and there were disputes over their independence in the mid-nineteenth century. During Gladstone's second Ministry of 1880–85, a compromise seemed to have been worked out: the Boers were effectively free to run their own affairs while in name they were under British sovereignty (overall control). But the discovery of prodigious mineral wealth in the area with the opening up of the Witwatersrand goldfield in the mid-1880s destroyed any chance that the British would leave their reluctant subjects alone. Outsiders (Uitlanders as the Boers called them) streamed into the Transvaal to participate in the gold mining. Many of these foreigners were British. The Boers – an isolated community of God-fearing cattle farmers – were not keen on being taken over by a variegated collection of mining prospectors and international capitalists. The Boer rulers in Transvaal ensured that while the incomers paid taxes they did not get normal civil and voting rights. Joseph Chamberlain, the Colonial Secretary from 1895 and Sir Alfred Milner, British High Commissioner in South Africa from 1897, both wanted to extend British imperial power and the Uitlanders' grievances presented them with an ideal reason to intervene in the Transvaal's internal affairs. Negotiations between Milner and the Transvaal's President, Paul Kruger, over Uitlanders' rights broke down (Milner never wanted them to succeed) and a subsequent Boer ultimatum in October 1899 opened the way for war. Why did Britain fight the second Boer War of 1899–1902?

A *From a letter from Chamberlain to Milner, 2 September 1899.*

It is a great thing to say that the majority of people have, as I believe, recognized that there is a greater issue than the franchise or the grievances of the Uitlanders at stake, and that our supremacy in S. Africa and our existence as a great power in the world are involved in the result of our present controversy. Three months ago we could not – that is to say we should not have been allowed to – go to war on this issue – now – although still most unwillingly and with a large minority still against us – we shall be sufficiently supported.

In: Porter A N 1980 *Joseph Chamberlain and the Diplomacy of Imperialism 1895–99* Manchester University Press, p 241

B *From Chamberlain's confidential Memorandum for the Cabinet on 'The South African Situation', 6 September 1899.*

What is now at stake is the position of Great Britain in South Africa – and with it the estimate formed of our power and influence in our Colonies and throughout the world.

... The contest for supremacy is between the Dutch and the English – the natives are interested spectators, with a preference for the English as their masters, but ready to take the side of the strongest ...

The Dutch in South Africa desire, if it be possible, to get rid altogether of the connection with Great Britain, which to them is not a motherland, and to substitute a United States of South Africa which, they hope, would be mainly under Dutch influence. This idea has always been present in their minds ... But it would probably have died out as a hopeless impossibility but for the evidence of successful resistance to British supremacy by the South African Republic. The existence of a pure Dutch Republic flouting, and flouting successfully, British control and interference, is answerable for all the racial animosities which have become so formidable a factor in the South African situation.

... Every one, natives included, sees that issue has been joined, and that it depends upon the action of the British Government now whether the supremacy, which we have claimed so long and so seldom exerted, is to be finally established and recognized or for ever abandoned.

This is, I repeat, the real question at stake. It has been simmering for years, and has now been brought to boiling point by a fortuitous combination of circumstances ...

I think that the object of the Government should now be to formulate its demands in a form to which a categorical yes or no may fairly be demanded.

I think the time has fully come when the troops in South Africa should be largely reinforced ...

PRO Cab 37/50/70. In: Grenville J A S 1964 *Lord Salisbury and Foreign Policy: The Close of the Nineteenth Century* Athlone Press, pp 257–8

C *The Prime Minister, Lord Salisbury, reports on the situation to Queen Victoria in the Cabinet Minutes, 23 September 1899.*

...we decline to admit that a small Dutch population shall be allowed in a state which is under Your Majesty's suzerainty to oppress a much larger number of Your Majesty's British subjects ... It is impossible to avoid believing that the Boers really aim at setting up a South African Republic, consisting of the Transvaal, the Orange Free State, and Your Majesty's Colony. It is impossible to account in any other manner for their rejection of our most moderate proposals.

PRO Cab 41/25/19

D *The Liberal Opposition leader, Henry Campbell-Bannerman, criticises government policy over the war.*

... Mr Chamberlain is mainly answerable for the war. It is the natural result of his persistent policy. Let me put it more fairly, it is one of the possible results of his persistent policy, not perhaps the result which he intended ... but still a natural result which he ought to have anticipated ...

The Times, 20 December 1899. In: *Speeches by the Rt Hon. Sir Henry Campbell-Bannerman*, selected and reprinted from *The Times*, 1908, p 40-1

E *The left-wing Liberal, J A Hobson, condemns the war.*

...We are fighting in order to place a small international oligarchy of mine-owners and speculators in power at Pretoria ...

The war is often described as press-made, but few of those who use this expression understand the all-important part which the great factory of public opinion has been made to play ... South Africa presents a unique example of a large press, owned, controlled, and operated in recent times by a small body of men with the direct aim of bringing about a conflict which shall serve their business interests.

Hobson J A 1900 *The War in South Africa* J Nisbet pp 197, 206

Questions

1 What was
 a 'Your Majesty's Colony' (Source C lines 8–9)?
 b 'Pretoria' (Source E line 3)?
2 What do Sources B and C suggest were the main reasons for the war? In what ways does Hobson give a different impression in Source E?
3 How do the sources suggest that public opinion was important in the conduct of diplomacy at this time?
4 How far do Sources B and C support Campbell-Bannerman's claim in Source D that 'Mr Chamberlain is mainly answerable for the war'?
5 From these sources and your own knowledge explain why Britain's 'existence as a great power in the world' was involved in the result of the controversy (Source A lines 5–6).[1]

Notes
1 See for example,
 Read D 1979 *England 1868-1914* Longman, Chap. 19
 Feuchtwanger E J 1985 *Democracy and Empire* Edward Arnold, Chap. 7
 Chamberlain M E 1974 *The Scramble for Africa* Longman, Chap. 6

12.2 Why Did Anglo-German Relations Deteriorate After 1900?

In the years 1898–99 the British government was involved in negotiations for an alliance with Germany, but a few years later the German government was viewed as a dangerous potential enemy. The *Entente Cordiale* (friendly understanding) with France in 1904 was of some significance in this as France was linked to Russia in a Dual Alliance which stood in opposition to the Triple Alliance of Germany, Austria-Hungary and Italy. Yet the *Entente Cordiale* did not itself imply any hostility towards Germany. Why did relations between Britain and Germany worsen so rapidly?

A *From a Cabinet Memorandum on the Naval estimates by the Conservative First Lord of the Admiralty Lord Selborne, October 1902.*

Since I wrote the two Memoranda for the Cabinet last autumn I have studied the naval policy of Germany more closely than I had previously done. The result of my study is that I am convinced that the great new German navy is being carefully built up from the point of view of a war with us. This is also the opinion of Sir Frank Lascelles, and he has authorised me to say so. The more the composition of the new German fleet is examined the clearer it becomes that it is designed for a possible conflict with the British fleet. It cannot be designed for the purpose of playing a leading part in a future war between Germany and France and Russia. The issue of such a war can only be decided by armies and on land, and the great naval expenditure on which Germany has embarked involves a deliberate diminution of the military strength which Germany might otherwise have attained in relation to France and Russia.

PRO Cab 37/63/142. In: Bourne K 1970 *The Foreign Policy of Victorian England 1830–1902* Oxford University Press, p 478

B *A cartoon from 'Punch', 1 November 1905*

THE SENSATIONAL PRESS.

BELLONA. "RUN AWAY, LITTLE BOYS, RUN AWAY! I WANT TO GO TO SLEEP."

C   *Extracts from articles about Germany by Bart Kennedy published in the 'Daily Mail', June 1906.*

For the last generation they (the German people) have been cowed and coerced by a gang of Prussian Huns – madmen, whose chief ambition was to disturb the world's peace so that they could show off the effect of a big conscript army. It is well to tell the English people the plain truth about this matter ...

Understand me. I am not blaming the German people. I say this again and again. I am only pointing out the fact that there is the danger of a small knot of Prussians forcing on one of the most horrible and desolating wars to be known in the history of mankind. And absolutely the only thing to influence this knot of Huns is force. They are amenable to no moral or intellectual influence. This is a terrible thing to say. But it is true.

Daily Mail, 8 and 13 June 1906. In: *'Scaremongerings' from the 'Daily Mail' 1896–1914*, pp 44–5

D   *From secret 'Memorandum on the present State of British Relations with France and Germany' by Eyre Crowe, Senior Clerk in the Foreign Office, January 1907.*

When the signature of the Algeciras Act brought to a close the first chapter of the conflict respecting Morocco, the Anglo-French *entente* had acquired a different significance from that which it had at the moment of its inception. Then there had been but a friendly settlement of particular outstanding differences, giving hope for future harmonious relations between two neighbouring countries that had got into the habit of looking at one another askance; now there had emerged an element of common resistance to outside dictation and aggression, a unity of special interests tending to develop into active co-operation against a third Power. It is essential to bear in mind that this new feature of the *entente* was the direct effect produced by Germany's effort to break it up, and that, failing the active or threatening hostility of Germany,

such anti-German bias as the *entente* must be admitted to have at one time assumed, would certainly not exist at present, nor probably survive in the future ...

PRO Cab 37/86/1. In: Gooch P G, Temperley H 1928 *British Documents on the Origins of the War*, H.M. Stationery Office, Vol. III, p 402

Questions

1 What was
  a 'the first chapter of the conflict respecting Morocco' (Source D lines 2–3)?
  b 'the Algeciras Act' (Source D line 1)?
2 How does Crowe argue that the first Moroccan conflict altered the nature of the *Entente Cordiale* in Source D?
3 What argument is put forward in Source B?
4 The extracts in Source C were reprinted after the start of World War I together with much other material to show that the *Daily Mail* had predicted the war. What is the value of these extracts to the historian?
5 Some have argued that World War I broke out more because of warlike diplomacy and popular misunderstandings than because of any irreconcilable conflict of interests between nations. How far could Sources A – D be used to support this argument?

12.3 Was Britain Committed to Join France in World War I?

Following the *Entente Cordiale* and the first Moroccan crisis of 1905–6, there were talks between British and French army officers to plan possible joint military operations in case their governments should decide on them in the future. Naval agreements followed in 1912-13, under which Britain concentrated her forces in Home waters and guarded the English Channel while

France looked after the defence of the Mediterranean. How far might these military arrangements commit Britain to join the French in a future war?

A *The Foreign Secretary, Sir Edward Grey, explains Britain's position in the House of Commons just before the outbreak of war.*

I come first, now, to the question of British obligations. I have assured the House ... that if any crisis such as this arose, we should come before the House of Commons and be able to say to the House that it was free to decide what the British attitude should be, that we would have no secret engagement which we should spring upon the House, and tell the House that, because we had entered into that engagement, there was an obligation of honour upon the country ... In this present crisis, up till yesterday, we have ... given no promise of anything more than diplomatic support ...

The French Fleet is now in the Mediterranean, and the Northern and Western coasts of France are absolutely undefended. The French fleet being concentrated in the Mediterranean the situation is very different from what it used to be, because the friendship which has grown up between the two countries has given them a sense of security that there was nothing to be feared from us. The French coasts are absolutely undefended. The French Fleet is in the Mediterranean, and has for some years been concentrated there because of the feeling of confidence and friendship which has existed between the two countries. My own feeling is that if a foreign fleet engaged in a war which France had not sought, and in which she had not been the aggressor, came down the English Channel and bombarded and battered the undefended coasts of France, we could not stand aside and see this going on practically within sight of our eyes, with our arms folded, looking on dispassionately, doing nothing! I believe that would be the feeling of this country ...

Hansard, 3 August 1914. Ser. 5, Vol. 65: 1810–16

B *Winston Churchill, the First Lord of the Admiralty, later described the situation.*

Sir Edward Grey ... authorized ... the beginning of military conversations between the British and French General Staffs with a view to concerted action in the event of war. This was a step of profound significance and of far-reaching reactions. Henceforward the relations of the two Staffs became increasingly intimate and confidential ... However explicitly the two Governments might agree and affirm to each other that no national or political engagement was involved in these technical discussions, the fact remained that they constituted an exceedingly potent tie ...

It is true to say that our Entente with France and the military and naval conversations that had taken place since 1906 had led us into a position where we had the obligations of an alliance without its advantages ...

Churchill W S 1923 *The World Crisis 1911–14*, Thornton Butterworth pp 32, 205

C *A French view of the discussions from General Huguet, French military attaché in London.*

It was understood that [the British Government] retained full liberty of action and that – if the likelihood of war between France and Germany were realised – the Government of the day would be the sole judge of the line of action to be taken, without being tied in any sense by the studies which might have been previously undertaken ... Nevertheless, we were somewhat surprised in 1906 to see the readiness with which the authorisation asked for by the French Government was granted. Sir Henry Campbell-Bannerman, Sir Edward Grey and Mr Haldane were all three, as politicians, too shrewd and wary not to realise that the studies which were being entered upon – no matter what the reservations – constituted nevertheless an undertaking of sorts, at any rate a moral one ...

General Huguet 1928, *Britain and the War: A French Indictment* Cassell, pp 5–6

D *R B Haldane, the Secretary for War, remembers the start of military staff negotiations in 1906.*

. . . The Prime Minister asked whether it could be made clear that the conversations were purely for military General Staff purposes and were not to prejudice the complete freedom of the two Governments should the situation the French dreaded arise. I undertook to see that this was put in writing . . . That the conversations were to leave us wholly free was expressed in a letter which was signed.

Haldane R B 1929 An Autobiography Hodder and Stoughton, p 190

E *Lord Riddell recorded a comment from a Cabinet minister, C F G Masterman, about a Cabinet meeting he attended before the declaration of war.*

. . . Grey had made it absolutely plain that unless France was supported, he would resign. On one occasion he remarked with great emotion, 'We have led France to rely upon us, and unless we support her in her agony, I cannot continue at the Foreign Office.'

Lord Riddell's War Diary 1914–1918. Nicholson and Watson, 1933, p 6

Questions

1 How far do Sources A and E suggest that Grey believed Britain had a moral obligation to help France in war?

2 Compare the views of Churchill and Huguet about the extent and nature of Britain's commitment to France in Sources B and C.

3 What are the problems in using
  a statesmen's memoirs as in Sources B and D?
  b second-hand accounts passed from one person to another as in Source E for a discussion of diplomatic and military obligations?

4 Do you think Britain was morally committed to support France in any defensive war against Germany?[1]

5 How significant was a moral commitment to France in determining Britain's entry into World War I and what other factors were important?[2]

Notes

1 For differing views see:
  Wilson T 'Britain's "Moral Commitment" to France in August 1914.' *History* October 1979
  Nicolson C 'Edwardian England and the Coming of the First World War.' In: O'Day A (ed) 1979 *The Edwardian Age Conflict and Stability 1900-1914* Macmillan
2 See text books and topic books, for example, Morgan M C 1973 *Foreign Affairs 1886-1914* Collins
  Chamberlain M E 1988 '*Pax Brittanica*'? *British Foreign Policy 1789-1914* Longman